Income and Inequality

INCOME AND INEQUALITY

The Role of the Service Sector in the Changing Distribution of Income

Cathy Kassab

Contributions in Economics and Economic History,
Number 133

Greenwood Press
New York • Westport, Connecticut • London

To
my parents, Jean and Lee Kassab,
for your loving support and encouragement
provided over the years

Library of Congress Cataloging-in-Publication Data

Kassab, Cathy.
  Income and inequality : the role of the service sector in the
changing distribution of income / Cathy Kassab.
      p.   cm. — (Contributions in economics and economic history,
  ISSN 0084-9235 ; no. 133)
    Includes bibliographical references and index.
    ISBN 0-313-27779-6 (alk. paper)
    1. Wages—Service industries—United States.   2. Income distribution—United
  States.   I. Title.   II. Series.
  HD4966.S452U522   1992
  331.2'81'000973—dc20   91-39642

British Library Cataloguing in Publication Data is available.

Library of Congress Catalog Card Number: 91-39642
ISBN: 0-313-27779-6
ISSN: 0084-9235

First published in 1992

Greenwood Press, 88 Post Road West, Westport, CT 06881
An imprint of Greenwood Publishing Group, Inc.

Printed in the United States of America

The paper used in this book complies with the Permanent Paper Standard issued by the National
Information Standards Organization (Z39.48-1984).

10 9 8 7 6 5 4 3 2 1

Copyright Acknowledgment

Material from "Studying Economic Change: Are Robust Regression Procedures Needed?" by
Cathy Kassab, appearing in *Rural Sociology*, vol. 55(3), 1990, reprinted by permission.

Contents

Figures and Tables

FIGURES

TABLES

Acknowledgments

This research is a result of advice given to me by my father. His concern for the economic well-being of people and increasing class divisions within communities and between rural and metropolitan centers led to his admonition that I study issues that are important to people living and working in small towns and rural areas. I would also like to thank my mother for all the assistance and encouragement she has provided throughout this process.

This research would not have been completed if it had not been for the help of several people. I would like to thank my husband, David Abler, for the assistance, support, and patience he has provided. His advice in the preparation of this manuscript has proven invaluable, and his thorough review of various drafts produced considerable improvements in the manuscript.

I would also like to thank my advisor and friend, Kenneth P. Wilkinson, for all the hours and energy he has spent teaching me to be critical and scholarly in my reasoning. He has trained me to think as a scientist and sociologist—I only hope I can continue to learn and follow his example. Also, I am very grateful to Rex Warland for the training he has provided in methodological and data analysis, and for the financial backing which enabled me to complete this research. Cliff Clogg, Larry Gamm, Al Luloff, and C. Shannon Stokes have also been instrumental in providing me with skills for attacking methodological and substantive problems. I would like to thank each of them for their attention to my training and work.

Claudio Frumento constructed the County Business Patterns and Bureau of Economic Analysis data base, while Tom Gesell prepared the Dun and Bradstreet data to fit the needs of the study. Their work proved to be essential to the research. Frank Goode provided me with access to various data sources, such as the Dun and Bradstreet files, and Al Luloff obtained the Bureau of Economic Analysis data. I would like to thank Leif Jensen for encouraging me to submit the original manuscript to Greenwood for review.

While this book could not have been produced without the assistance and support of those mentioned, I claim responsibility for all material presented here.

Income and Inequality

1

Issues and Trends

The objective of this book is to examine the impact of increasing service sector employment on social well-being. The changing composition of local and regional economies, and the effect these changes have on earnings, the quality of jobs, and the standard of living in the United States have spawned interest in this topic.

Both urban and rural places in the United States have experienced a reduction in the growth rate of manufacturing employment, while increasing their reliance on the service sector for employment (Brown and Deavers, 1987:3–5; Menchik, 1981:232, Table 1). Employment growth among service-producing industries between 1972 and 1986 was 57.9 percent, compared with 4.3 percent for goods-producing industries (Kutscher, 1987:Table 2).[1]

But between 1973 and 1988, weekly wages declined across the nation from $308 to $277, and median family income fell from $27,072 in 1973 to $25,738 in 1985 (in constant 1982–84 dollars) (Population Today, 1988:3). Some have blamed the shift from manufacturing to services for this decline in wages, since earnings in manufacturing tend to be higher than those in services (*Population Today*, 1988:3; Sternlieb and Hughes, 1984:77–82).

For instance, gross weekly earnings in 1988 were $331 in manufacturing but $225 in services (in constant 1982 dollars) (Sternlieb and Hughes, 1984:xxi). In addition, the service sector is characterized by a preponderance of part-time positions, paying lower wages with little or no health or retirement benefits (Appelbaum and Albin, 1990:46–50). Differences in these factors, combined with stagnation and growth in the two sectors, respectively, are often used to explain a substantial portion of the decline in income (Sternlieb and Hughes, 1984:73–91).[2]

Several issues have been raised regarding the ability of the service sector to fuel the local economy and to promote equality of access to resources. One concern is that the service sector will be unable to provide the number of "family wage" jobs which the locality previously sustained or would be expected from development of the nonservice sector. Some expect this transition to result in a decrease in aggregate resources in the community (Gruenstein and Guerra, 1981; Marquand, 1979; Oregon Joint Legislative Committee on Trade and Economic Development, 1984:3, 15; Pulver, 1986c).

Another concern is that a concurrent loss of middle-income manufacturing jobs combined with an increase in lower- and higher-wage-paying service sector jobs will result in the income distribution becoming bifurcated (that is, more bipolarized) (Browne, 1986:24, Table 4; McMahon and Tschetter, 1986:22). This type of trend implies that declines occur in the middle income group while the lower and upper income groups increase in number (see Browne, 1986:24, Table 4).

Increasing disparities in income between those in the lower income group and the remainder of the population result in solidified barriers that separate people at different levels of the income distribution. Relatedly, there are fears that changes in the industrial mix away from manufacturing and towards services will result in the development of a two-tiered class structure, or a decrease in the opportunities for advancement among those at the bottom of the income distribution (Appelbaum and Albin, 1990; Rosenthal, 1985:3). A third concern is that disparities between rural and urban communities will increase as industries providing professional, technical, and managerial services locate primarily in more urbanized areas (Gillespie and Green, 1987).

The viability of local and regional economies is directly related to the level of social well-being characterizing a place. Social well-being is concerned with those social conditions which promote the welfare of individuals. At one level, social well-being refers to the welfare or stability of the community (Lincoln and Friedland, 1977:306; Wilkinson, 1979:9). Whether the community is able to sustain itself over time affects the social well-being of its members. Higher levels of social well-being are promoted by the efficient operation of the community, implying the capability to obtain optimum return to the community as a whole (Pulver, 1986a:10). Thus, one aspect of social well-being is the availability of resources for creating an adequate sustenance organization. Both the individual and locality require these resources to be available in order for well-being to be maintained.

A second aspect of social well-being is the extent to which there is an equitable distribution of resources (Pulver, 1986a:10; Smith, 1974; Wilkinson, 1979:14–15). Equity is a value judgment in which the fairness of the distribution of resources is at issue. At the individual level, the concept of equity can be related to the presence of social barriers within the community. Furthermore, social barriers can separate communities if resources are inequitably distributed across geographic space (Smith, 1974:292, 295).

These barriers inhibit achieving one's potentials by suppressing participation in events that build and maintain the community structure and its relationship with external agencies (Wilkinson, 1979:10, 15). Inequalities derived from structural arrangements existing within or between localities, such as societal stratification systems, result in various groups having differential access to resources. Inequality of access is one form by which the distribution of resources becomes inequitable. As a result, the well-being of groups with reduced access is expected to be restricted by the presence of social and economic barriers (Wilkinson, 1979:7).

Varying levels of dependence on the manufacturing and service sectors can affect a community's social well-being through wage rates. As wages change, the aggregate level of income in the community is affected, as well as the distribution of income in the community. Growth in lower- and higher-wage service sector jobs, occurring simultaneously with declines in middle- and higher-wage manufacturing jobs, is expected to affect the distribution of income in the community. The position of the community in a hierarchy of communities, based on aggregate income in the community, will be affected by changes in the community's industrial mix if these changes vary by the position of the community in that hierarchy.

DEFINITIONS AND TRENDS

Service sector activities have been characterized as activities which are intangible, ephemeral, or not directly involved with processing physical materials. Human capital is often said to be of greater importance in the production of services than physical capital. However, this description of services is inaccurate when applied to actual cases. For instance, many communication and distribution services are capital intensive (Marshall, 1988:11–12). Communication involves telephone lines; trading and selling information is dependent on physical capital such as computers, fax machines, and other high-technology equipment. Medical services also rely on physical capital, such as wheelchairs and X-ray machines.

Because of the diversity of activities included under the rubric of "services," this sector is often defined on the basis of exclusion from other activities. For instance, services do not include agriculture, mining, or manufacturing. This approach to defining services is ultimately unsatisfactory, since characteristics distinguishing services remain unspecified. In order to develop meaningful categories, we need to go beyond simply collapsing all service activities into a single group.

A more appropriate categorization distinguishes between service industries interconnected with the goods-producing sector and services not directly connected to the goods-producing process, but rather serving consumers. These two categories are commonly referred to as producer and consumer services, respectively.

Producer services, in the same way as manufacturing industries, supply primarily business firms and governmental agencies, rather than individuals. These services can be directly traded among or within organizations. They have economic value because they contribute to the competitiveness of another industry. As a result of the combination of these characteristics, producer services are considered part of the supply capacity of the economy. This means that they help determine the response and adjustment of the economy to changing conditions (Marshall, 1988:13).

The types of services falling under the rubric of producer services include financial, legal, general management, innovation, development, design, administration, personnel, production technology, maintenance, transport, communication, wholesale distribution, advertising, and selling (Marshall, 1988:13–16). Industries corresponding to this definition include finance, insurance, and real estate (FIRE), business services, legal services, membership organizations, and professional services (Noyelle, 1986a:Table 7.1).[3]

On the other hand, principal markets for consumer and retail service firms are private individuals. Firms classified as consumer services include retail stores, restaurants, hotels and other lodging places, personal services, and auto repair and services (Noyelle, 1986a: Table 7.1; Miller and Bluestone, 1987: Table 2).

A classification scheme related to the producer/consumer dichotomy categorizes firms by whether they possess an export orientation. Export-oriented firms are an avenue through which new monies enter the local economy, thereby providing the means for economic growth to occur (Smith, 1984). An export orientation means that services produced by the firm are sold to markets outside the local economy, thereby bringing extralocal income into it. As with the producer services, export-oriented firms have a tendency not to serve individuals directly (Porterfield, 1989:19). While economic development strategies have focused on attracting export-oriented manufacturing firms, producer service firms also have been found to exhibit an export orientation (Beyers and Alvine, 1985; Smith, 1984).

However, locally owned export-oriented firms are better able to contribute to the economic growth and development of the community than externally controlled firms. This latter group of firms is not as likely to purchase inputs locally, or to take the needs and interest of the locality into consideration when making decisions (Glasmeier and Borchard, 1989; Smith, 1984). But in rural areas, export-oriented firms are less likely to be under local ownership, so the potential of these firms to contribute to the local economy rural places is reduced (Smith, 1984).

It should be noted that consumer and retail services appear to have some capabilities for infusing extralocal dollars into local economies, particularly in rural areas (Gillis, 1987; Marquand, 1979). In many rural communities a substantial proportion of residents in a community rely upon money drawn on extralocal banks, such as the elderly receiving Social Security and pension benefits checks. Because local income multipliers are induced by purchases with extralocal dollars, consumer service firms, such as restaurants and retail stores, can serve as a point through which extralocal resources enter the local economy (Gillis, 1987:250–51).[4]

Employment in most types of services is exhibiting rapid growth, as portrayed in Figure 1.1. Between 1970 and 1988, employment in business and legal services increased by nearly 236 percent, or approximately 4.7 million jobs. Finance, insurance, and real estate (FIRE) added another 3 million jobs (83 percent increase), while health services increased by 4.1 million (134 percent increase).[5] Job growth in the consumer services added at least another 8.2 million jobs (68.5 percent increase). Moreover, these same industries are expected to continue growing at least until the year 2000. In contrast, manufacturing employment grew only slightly (0.2 percent) between 1970 and 1988, with little change expected to occur through the year 2000 (U.S. Bureau of the Census, 1990: Table 651). A detailed description of the income potential of jobs in various service sector industries is presented in the second chapter.

WHY THE TRANSITION TO SERVICES

This description of trends begs the question of why this shift in employment has occurred. Several reasons have been proposed as an explanation for the rapid growth in service sector employment.

Some of the rise in service sector employment has been attributed to goods-producing firms "unbundling" or transferring certain service activities from in-house to outside firms. Employment growth stemming from this source is only apparent rather than real, since activities are simply being transferred between organizations (Tschetter, 1987). However, evidence indicates that unbundling by the manufacturing sector constituted only a small portion of the employment growth in producer services from 1972 to 1986 in the United States (Tschetter, 1987).

Other reasons for the growth in service sector employment include low productivity associated with the service sector in comparison to the goods-producing sector, the expansion of not-for-profit institutions such as government, and increasing demand for services due to changing business practices, increasing consumer preference for services over goods, and growth in international trade in services (Ginzberg and Vojta, 1981; Noyelle, 1990; Office of Technology Assessment, 1986; Stanback and Noyelle, 1990; Tschetter, 1987).

Simply presented, the low-productivity hypothesis states that certain subsectors of the service sector are "stagnant," meaning these subsectors are labor-intensive, with technology having limited applicability. Productivity levels are relatively constant over time and as a result lag behind more "progressive" sectors in the economy (Stanback and Noyelle, 1990:199–201). This hypothesis proposes that the higher wages being earned in the more productive or progressive sector would eventually spread to the stagnant sector. Costs and prices from the stagnant sector would increase likewise, to account for higher wages without associated gains in productivity. Gradually the stagnant sector absorbs a larger portion of

Figure 1.1
Employment in Selected Industries

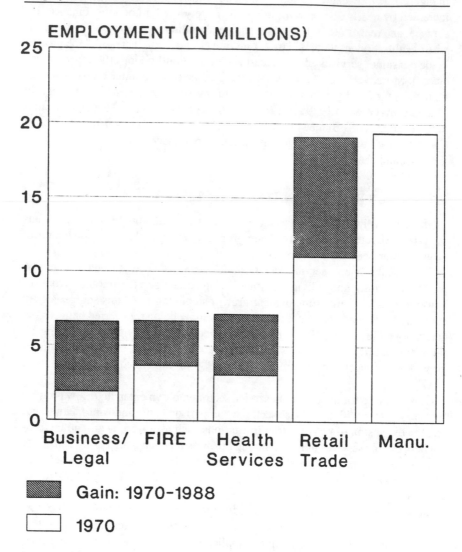

EMPLOYMENT (IN MILLIONS)

Business/Legal FIRE Health Services Retail Trade Manu.

Gain: 1970-1988

1970

Source: U.S. Bureau of the Census, 1990

employment in the total economy (Stanback and Noyelle, 1990:199–201). Continuing this line of thought, deindustrialization would occur as higher-paying jobs in manufacturing are lost and increasing numbers of (lower-paying) jobs become available in those service industries unlikely to undergo gains in productivity (Stanback and Noyelle, 1990:204).

The major problem with assessing the evidence for this hypothesis is that measures of productivity for many industries in the service sector do not accurately measure change in productivity. Productivity is defined as a measure of output to a measure of input, generally labor. However, due to the lack of an output measure for many service industries, a labor input measure, such as weighted labor hours, is used to measure output in the sector. In these cases productivity will not change much over time since the numerator and denominator are so closely related (that is, both are input measures) (Stanback and Noyelle, 1990:188–90, 201). Furthermore, comparing measures of productivity over time between goods-producing and service industries would be of questionable validity, due to the insensitivity of productivity measures to change among service industries. Hence, given current methods of data collection on the service sector, we are unable to accurately assess the level of productivity and changes in it for many of its industries.

In contrast to the unbundling and low-productivity explanations, the other reasons listed above tend to focus on the positive contributions of the service sector to the economy to explain its growth. For instance, changes in business practices (other than unbundling), result from increased demand for information and knowledge-based services. Gains in physical capital can occur as a result of effectively accessing human capital skills, particularly in the producer services among organizations in advanced economies. An industry that relies on service activities to increase its competitive position by advertising in the various media or to develop necessary computer software are two examples (Ginzberg and Vojta, 1981:5; Tschetter, 1987:38).

Relatedly, the increased demand for professional and technical services provided by lawyers, accountants, business managers, and so on, may be occurring in response to increasing numbers and complexity of corporations, as well as the volume of government laws and regulations (Tschetter, 1987:38).

Increasing consumer demand for services in the United States may be due to the wide and highly differentiated market for products and services (Stanback and Noyelle, 1990:205). Consistent with increasing differentiation in the market, increasing numbers of women entering the work force, such as those with families, create a demand for support services that would have been performed by a housewife working at home (Ginzberg and Vojta, 1981:53). Consumer services such as child care, laundry, or eating and drinking services are examples of industries likely to benefit.

The expansion of the not-for-profit sector, particularly government, has resulted also in increasing growth in service employment. The not-for-profit sector provides the major impetus for developing human capital, in the form of expenditures for higher education, as well as research and development in high-technology fields such as defense and space. Due to expenditures by government and many nonprofit organizations, such as nonprofit insurance companies (for example, Blue Cross–Blue Shield), the health care system has grown (Ginzberg and Vojta, 1981:51–52).

International trade, particularly in business services such as transportation, travel, and licensing, is another source of growth in the service sector (Office of Technology Assessment, 1986).[6] The Office of Technology Assessment (OTA) (1986) estimated that between 1982 and 1984 services made a net positive contribution to the balance of payments, (that is, exports exceeded imports). Furthermore, OTA reported that the surplus in net exports of services was underestimated (at the midrange) by $11 billion in 1982 and 1983 and $12 billion in 1984 (OTA, 1986:8–9).[7]

The place of services in the global marketplace is highlighted by the necessity of a well-laid infrastructure in services for economic growth in both developed and developing countries (Riddle, 1987). The importance of service trade tends to be greater for developed countries, however, where services constitute a larger proportion of total trade in these countries (Riddle, 1987:95). For instance, the United States holds a larger share of world exports in international services trade (21.5 percent in 1984) than in merchandise trade (12.7 percent in 1984) (Landefeld and Young, 1988:96–97). However, the U.S. share of exports in services and merchandise trade dropped two to three percentage points between 1970 and 1984 as other countries expanded their international trade in services (Landefeld and Young, 1988:96–97).

The increasing importance of international services trade has resulted in a push, particularly by the United States, for the General Agreement on Tariffs and Trade (GATT) to include rules for international trade in services as well as for goods (Feketekuty, 1988:85). Trade in services constitutes one-fifth of total world trade (Farnsworth, 1990). Currently, there is no framework for defining fair international trade practices in services or for settling disputes across countries (Farnsworth, 1990; Feketekuty, 1988). However, a need clearly exists for a framework to govern international trade in services. For instance, the International Trade Commission estimated that U.S. businesses lose at least $60 billion a year from theft of intellectual property, such as ideas used to create products such as computer software or pharmaceuticals being pirated (Farnsworth, 1990).

COMMON (MIS)CONCEPTIONS OF THE
SERVICE SECTOR

The importance of services in the local, regional, and global economy has traditionally been overlooked (Riddle, 1986). Several popular misconceptions about the service sector have contributed to services being undervalued as a resource for sustaining the economy. This sector has a more positive impact on the economy than is generally thought.

The Fisher-Clark classification of industries into sectors provides one source by which negative conceptions of service activities have been formed. Fisher referred to the service sector as tertiary, while Clark referred to industries in this sector as the residual category. Both schemes result in a heterogeneous array of industries being clumped into a single category (Riddle, 1986:2–5), and this makes it difficult to ascertain the positive contributions services might make to the economy.

Another misconception regarding the service sector arises from referring to growth in the sector as part of the postindustrial transformation of society. This terminology suggests that a certain degree of capital development is necessary before an economy can depend on services, and that service sector growth occurs after labor moves into manufacturing. But this generalization does not appear to hold across several important cases. In the United States and Canada, developments in manufacturing occurred simultaneously with transformations in capital markets, transportation, and communication. Developments in services permitted the transformation of the manufacturing process to occur as it did. And in Japan, labor moved into services prior to manufacturing (Riddle, 1986:6–7).

A third source of bias against the service sector is the preference for capital-intensive industries over labor-intensive ones as sources of economic development; productivity is assumed to be higher in capital-intensive industries. In fact, while the service sector is often considered labor-intensive, rapid improvements in production techniques have occurred over the last three decades, due to advances in areas such as automatic data processing, telecommunications, and achievements in economies of scale (for example, advent of supermarkets) (Marquand, 1979:33).

Furthermore, traditional distinctions between manufacturing and services no longer apply to many of the industries in these sectors. For one, the output of manufactured products is becoming increasingly interdependent with the service sector. Manufacturing industries do not simply provide the demand that is supplied by service industries. The various sectors of the economy are interdependent, and services can also stimulate manufacturing growth (Marshall, 1988:3–5; Riddle, 1986:21–28).

For example, in the manufacture of data processing equipment, computer software is an input provided by the service sector. Software affects the success of the product on the market, as well as being necessary for the product to function (Marshall, 1988:4). In addition, service sector industries purchased over 80 percent of the computers, office equipment, and communications equipment in the United States in 1982, thereby providing a market for these service industries (Riddle, 1986:25).

A second area in which the distinction has blurred is in the delineation of markets for service and manufacturing industries. The different sectors appear to be interpenetrating each other's market. The newspaper industry is a case in point. Newspaper production is part of the manufacturing sector, but that industry competes with radio and television broadcasts, both members of the service sector (Marshall, 1988:4).

Third, service and manufacturing industries can no longer be differentiated based on the capital versus labor-intensive dichotomy. A variety of different types of service industries are becoming increasingly capital-intensive, such as financial services, communications, and health care (Marshall, 1988:3–5).

POSTINDUSTRIAL AND DEINDUSTRIALIZATION PERSPECTIVES

Two views often pitted against each other in the literature focusing on the implications of the transition to a service-based or service-oriented economy are the postindustrial and the deindustrialization perspectives. The postindustrial view emphasizes the central role of professional and technical occupations and, accordingly, education in managing an economy based upon services. The implications of the postindustrial perspective for short- and long-term social well-being are mixed. On one hand, this perspective implies that increased demand for a more educated work force will result in educational levels of the general populace rising. Accordingly, some feel that educational inequality should decrease (Blau, 1980).

Women have traditionally faced barriers to obtaining employment in extractive industries, construction, and durable manufacturing, but these barriers have become less of an obstacle as an increasing proportion of jobs becomes available in services (Appelbaum and Albin, 1990:51; Browne, 1986). Women have increasingly entered the labor force as the number of jobs in the service sector have increased. It is true that many of the positions filled by women are lower-level, low-paying jobs (Stanback and Noyelle, 1982). Evidence from the 1980 census indicates, however, that gaps in earnings and occupational achievements have narrowed somewhat between men and women in metropolitan areas with increased employment in services (Lorence, 1991).

Also, racial barriers to occupational mobility, while still evident, appear to have decreased over time (Blau, 1980). One study reports, using 1980 census data, that higher levels of employment in the producer services are associated with a greater range of employment opportunities for black men and women living in metropolitan areas (Bloomquist, 1990:210). Other research indicates that producer services in which blacks have increased their share of the work force to the greatest extent include FIRE and business services (Appelbaum and Albin, 1990:52). Gaps, however, persist in the proportion of minority groups receiving training considered necessary for obtaining employment. Black workers are less likely than white workers to receive training needed to qualify for their job (Stacey and To, 1990:177).

So while the postindustrial perspective implies that women and minority groups will make some gains, barriers which prevent these groups from obtaining increased earnings and occupational mobility still remain. Also, the implications of the postindustrial perspective for the level and distribution of income are not clear

(Blau, 1980), due to the prevalence of both lower- and higher-paying jobs in the service sector. Overall, however, the postindustrial approach provides a fairly optimistic view of the transition to a service-based economy. The long-term trend is for a more educated work force, in which gender and racial barriers are expected to gradually diminish.

On the other hand, the deindustrialization perspective focuses on the economic implications of a long-term decrease in manufacturing employment (Marshall, 1988:33). The transition to a service-based economy is viewed as a consequence of the erosion of the industrial base and a loss of competitiveness in the international marketplace as manufactured imports exceed exports (Kutscher and Personick, 1986; Marshall, 1988:33).[8]

According to this perspective, the economic consequences of the transition are expected to be negative, as workers are forced to substitute lower-wage work in services for higher-paying jobs in manufacturing. The result is an economy built around low-wage, low-productivity employment (Appelbaum and Albin, 1990; Lorence, 1991; Marshall, 1988). In addition, since the service sector is characterized by a substantial portion of part-time jobs with few health or retirement benefits (Appelbaum and Albin, 1990; U.S. GAO, 1991), the need for publicly funded social welfare programs, such as a national health insurance, will increase as this proportion of the work force increases.

The implications of this view for short- and long-term social well-being are fairly negative. The income distribution is expected to become more bifurcated as jobs in the low- and high-paying service sector continue to replace middle-income jobs in manufacturing. The standard of living for those in the lower income group would continue to erode as opportunities for advancement disappear. As a result, society would become increasingly stratified. Education and training in professional, technical, or managerial areas would be required for experiencing gains in the standard of living and occupational mobility.

Hopefully, this brief introduction to the role of services in the economy communicates the growing importance of this sector to the United States and world economy. However, the dearth of statistical information on economic activity in various service industries is complemented by our lack of knowledge regarding the impact of growth in this sector on social well-being.

RELEVANCE OF STUDYING THE LOCALITY

I am focusing this study at the community level, rather than on families, regions, or nations, for several reasons. Major issues examined in this book deal with the impact of increasing service sector employment on income and its distribution. The community can be viewed as a relatively complete social grouping for meeting one's daily needs (Hawley, 1950:257–58). Issues and problems affecting our lives occur within the context of this local settlement area. For example, whether a community has enough resources to maintain public institutions such as schools, or infrastructures like sewage and water systems, affects the well-being of its members.

Further, there is a growing awareness that local differences among communities exist within the same region (Bradley and Lowe, 1984:7–13). These differences can be important for assessing differences in the welfare of the community (Goode, 1985:190). So communities differ, even within the same region, in their capacity to provide resources for maintaining the well-being of their members.

Relatedly, service sector growth may affect rural places differently than urban ones. Studies documenting employment trends in the United States from 1969 to 1984 and in Britain from 1971 to 1981 have found that a major source of service sector growth in smaller places is in the lower-wage retail and consumer services. Conversely, higher-paying producer services tend to locate in larger urban centers (Gillespie and Green, 1987; Miller and Bluestone, 1987; Noyelle and Stanback, 1983). Hence, many feel that disparities will increase among communities located at opposite ends of the population size spectrum if rural communities and metropolitan centers experience growth in economic sectors differing in income potentials (Gillespie and Green, 1987:400–401, 403–6; Miller and Bluestone, 1987:10–15; Stanback and Noyelle, 1982:50).

METHODOLOGICAL AND STATISTICAL DESIGN

Two separate samples are used in the analyses described in this manuscript. In order to conduct a detailed study of the influence of industrial and demographic changes on income and its distribution, communities in the Mid-Atlantic region of the United States (New Jersey, New York, and Pennsylvania) during the 1970–80 decade constitute one sample.[9] The communities, comprised of an urban area and associated hinterland, are similar to the concept of community area used by Hawley (1950:245–63) in which residents are functionally interdependent over a contiguous geographic space. The method by which the communities were created is described in Appendix A.

The reason why this sample is used is that the Mid-Atlantic region underwent a transition from dependency on the goods-producing sector to the service sector during the 1970–1980 period. Both metropolitan and nonmetropolitan areas in the Mid-Atlantic experienced a restructuring in their economic base (Fuller, 1986: Table 9; Noyelle, 1986a:151; Noyelle and Stanback, 1983:2; Sternlieb and Hughes, 1978:9; Till, 1981:197), thereby making the region during this period an appropriate context for the study sample. Most of the attention in this book focuses on the Mid-Atlantic sample.

Income, population, and other demographic data used in the analysis of the Mid-Atlantic sample are from the U.S. Census of Population and Housing for 1970 and 1980. Dun and Bradstreet files for 1968 and 1979 provide employment data on service and manufacturing firms.

In addition, an analysis of recent trends is conducted using a sample of all counties in the United States for the late 1970s to late 1980s.[10] Updating the analysis lets us observe whether similar trends are evident across the two decades. Income data for 1979 and 1988 are from the Bureau of Economic Analysis (BEA) data files, while employment data for 1978 and 1987 are from County Business Patterns (CBP). Also, differences in wage rates between manufacturing and service sector industries in metropolitan and nonmetropolitan counties for 1987 are examined with data from CBP.

A variety of statistical procedures are used in the analysis. For example, robust regression analysis is used to control for the influence of outliers among the explanatory variables. Other statistical procedures used to supplement analyses include cluster analysis and canonical correlation analysis.

The following paragraphs contain a summary of the issues covered in the chapters that follow. The second chapter presents a review of the empirical research dealing with the association between employment in services and income. The third chapter describes the sample and model used in the analysis of communities in the Mid-Atlantic region, while the fourth chapter presents the results. The analysis of county-level trends in the entire United States between 1978 and 1988 is reported in the fifth chapter. Implications of the analyses for social policy are discussed in the last chapter.

Several appendices follow the main text. Appendix A contains technical details on defining and operationalizing the concept of community, while Appendix B provides a detailed discussion of the measurement issues involved in using employment data from the Dun and Bradstreet files. Appendix C reports results of an analysis justifying the use of family income, rather than income from all units in the community, to measure the dependent variables in the Mid-Atlantic region. A descriptive analysis of change in the distribution of income among communities in the Mid-Atlantic region during the 1969–1979 period is presented in Appendix D. Appendix E reports results from the cluster analysis used to create variables measuring the industrial mix of the community, while Appendix F contains results from a supplementary analysis of income inequality measures. Appendix G is a technical discussion of statistical procedures used in the analyses. Additional tables are provided in Appendix H.

NOTES

1. This data was prepared by the Bureau of Labor Statistics. Goods-producing industries include mining, construction, and manufacturing. Service-producing industries include transportation, public utilities, wholesale trade, retail trade, finance, insurance, real estate, and services (Kutscher, 1987: Table 2).

2. Age-related earning differentials is another factor used to explain the decline in wages. The number of workers under 25 years in the work force was at a peak during the 1970s. This group typically earns less than those over 25 years (Sternlieb and Hughes, 1984:80–81).

3. The distributive services, which include transportation, communications and utilities, and wholesale trade, serve to transport various goods and services among producer firms, as well as to transport outputs from producer to consumer firms (Noyelle,

1986a:147). Also, services such as health care, while not considered a producer service, bring extralocal dollars into the community from sources such as government and private insurance (Gruenstein and Guerra, 1981).

4. However, the potential of the consumer service sector to propel the local economy tends to be far below that of the producer service sector (Glasmeier and Borchard, 1989: 1574). Employment among the consumer service industries tends to be low-paying, so the multiplier effects from this source may be small (Hoppe, 1991).

Further, the demand for consumer services is likely to stabilize or decrease in the future. Consumer service industries have grown due to increased demand and disposable income. Higher rates of women participating in the labor force and increased numbers of retired persons with an adequate income have contributed to this trend. But, the rate by which women continue to enter the labor force is expected to reach a maximum and stabilize. Also, benefit and retirement packages are being reduced, resulting in a decrease in the number of retired persons with adequate pensions (Glasmeier and Borchard, 1989:1574). Further, the potential contribution of consumer services is largest in rural and isolated areas where markets for these services have not been saturated (Gillis, 1987; Marquand, 1979). But, the elderly in rural areas are more likely to be poor, so the amount of disposable income is at a minimum (Hoppe, 1991). The stability of the Social Security system is also a factor to be considered in the long term, since Social Security contributes about one-third of an elderly person's income, with that contribution being about two thirds among the rural elderly. Given the current payroll tax rate, the Social Security trust fund is expected to become a deficit in 2051 (Hoppe, 1991:14).

5. It should be noted, however, that some service industries, such as real estate, did experience a minor decline in employment due to the recessions during the 1980s (Plunkert, 1990:14).

6. Actually, investment income has provided the largest contribution to U.S. exports; this includes interest, dividends, and profits on foreign investments. Other service activities contributing significantly to U.S. exports are business services such as travel, transportation, royalties, and fees. Government services, such as arms sales and defense expenditures, also constitute a major portion of U.S. service exports (Landefeld and Young, 1988:91–94). Sales of services through foreign affiliates of U.S. corporations is at least as important in international service trade as direct exports of services; these activities are not, however, recorded in the balance of payments (Landefeld and Young, 1988:94).

7. Inadequate procedures for gathering and analyzing statistical data on trade and investment in services result in a large degree of uncertainty over the balance of payments for services. For instance, OTA estimated that the balance of payments for services in 1984 ranges from a deficit of $4 billion to a surplus of $32 billion, with the mid-range estimate being $14 billion. The Bureau of Economic Analysis, the federal agency responsible for calculating the balance of payments, estimated the surplus at $2.3 billion (OTA, 1986:9, 15).

8. The view that the United States is actually losing its manufacturing base has been contended. Kutscher and Personick (1986) found that many manufacturing industries are increasing productivity, thereby allowing the production of goods to increase without an increase in employment. Also, the shift away from manufacturing-based employment to services has been relative rather than absolute, meaning the numbers employed in manufacturing have remained fairly constant while the number employed in services has increased (Kutscher and Personick, 1986).

9. All communities in the region, except New York City and Philadelphia, are included in the sample.

10. The analysis using the sample of communities in the Mid-Atlantic region was not updated to 1990 since the appropriate U.S. Census data for 1990 was not yet available.

2

Service Employment and Income: A Survey of the Literature

The following topics are relevant to our understanding of how changes in the structure of employment are affecting income and its distribution:

- How does growth in the service sector affect the community income level and its distribution,
- How do changes in the industrial mix of communities affect the distribution of income across places, and
- How does the impact of the service sector on income compare with that of manufacturing?

The studies reviewed in this chapter provide a synopsis of our understanding of the impact of changes in local economies, particularly in the service sector, on community income levels and their distribution. Since the purpose of this research is to provide input into policy on local economic development, a more complete understanding of the impact of change in the service sector can be achieved by comparing its effect with that of other dominant sectors in the local economy, such as manufacturing.

The most direct way to achieve this goal is to draw primarily from empirical analyses of the problem. Theories from sociology and economics have been used indirectly as a basis for ordering empirical analyses into a conceptually integrated framework for examining the problem.

EARNINGS IN THE SERVICE SECTOR

Much of our knowledge about services and their relationship to income is provided by analyses of employment and earnings trends. The variety of industries in the service sector is complemented by the wide range of weekly earnings associated with different jobs in the sector. The service sector is characterized by both low-paying unskilled and semiskilled jobs and high-paying professional and technical jobs (Danziger, 1976:472–74; Nelson and Lorence, 1988; Oregon Joint Legislative Committee on Trade and Economic Development, 1984; Stanback and Noyelle, 1982:29–51).

While there appears to be a steady supply of new jobs into the local economy, those provided by consumer and retail trade industries tend to be low-paying. Annual earnings tend to be low across all occupations in these industries, although this may be partially a result of the large number of part-time workers (Stanback and Noyelle, 1982:48, Table 3.9). For example, 57 percent of the workers in retail trade earned between 40 percent and 80 percent of the U.S. average earnings per worker, and 65.4 percent of those employed in consumer services made less than 40 percent of the U.S. average.[1] (Stanback and Noyelle, 1982:33).

Jobs in finance, insurance, and real estate (FIRE) tend to follow a bifurcated earnings structure. While approximately 50 percent of those employed in the industry earn at least 1.2 times the national average, essentially the other half of the workers were paid between 0.4 and 0.8 times the national average (Stanback and Noyelle, 1982: Table 3.3).

Conversely, the earnings distribution in wholesale trade is more similar to that of manufacturing than other rapidly growing service industries. Both are characterized by medium-wage jobs. Nearly 80 percent of those employed in wholesale trade earned at least 0.8 times the U.S. average, while over 85 percent employed in manufacturing earned this much. No workers employed in manufacturing earned less than 0.4 times the national average, while only 1 percent of the employees in wholesale trade did (Stanback and Noyelle, 1982: Table 3.3). However, wholesale trade has a greater proportion of workers in the highest income categories and less in the middle-income group. The top-heaviness of the income distribution for wholesale trade is evidenced by 48.5 percent earning at least 1.6 times the U.S. average, while 20 percent in manufacturing earned at least this much (Stanback and Noyelle, 1982: Table 3.3).

Additional evidence of a bifurcated earnings structure in the service sector is provided by data listing the share of part-time employment within high- and low-paying service industries.[2] Part-time employment constitutes only 27 percent and 33 percent of the share of employment in wholesale trade and FIRE, respectively. These percentages are similar to those for manufacturing (32 percent). On the other hand, some of the highest percentages of employees working part-time are found in retail and consumer services (55 percent and 64 percent, respectively). The large number of part-time employees in these industries reinforces the lower level of earnings associated with this group (Stanback and Noyelle, 1982:48, Table 3.9).

These trends suggest that increasing service sector employment will result in a bifurcated earnings structure due to the shortage of middle-income jobs. For instance, between 1960 and 1975, earnings in the U.S. labor force became more bifurcated as a result of nearly 90 percent of the new jobs in services occurring among those earning either less than 80 percent of the national average or at least 120 percent of the national average. Increasing employment in service, combined with internal occupational shifts in service and goods-producing industries has lead to these changes (Stanback and Noyelle, 1982:38–39: Table 3.5).

Bipolarization of the income distribution would lead to increasing disparities between those in the lower income group and the remainder of the population; inequality is expected to rise as a result (Bluestone and Harrison, 1987; Browne, 1986; Nelson and Lorence, 1988; Oregon Joint Legislative Committee on Trade and Economic Development, 1984). Thus these changes could promote the development of a two-tiered class structure or a loss in opportunities for advancement among those at the bottom of the income distribution (Rosenthal, 1985:3). Furthermore, since women fill many of the lowest-paying positions in the service sector, a decrease in opportunities for those in the lower income groups will result in many women facing increased barriers to economic well-being (Appelbaum and Albin, 1990).

ANALYZING THE RELATIONSHIP BETWEEN SERVICE SECTOR GROWTH AND COMMUNITY INCOME

A sobering picture is presented when these trends are examined from the community or regional level of analysis. The service sector has been increasing its share of total employment, while the goods-producing sectors, which include manufacturing and agriculture, have been declining for decades (Gruenstein and Guerra, 1981:16). For instance, in 1979 manufacturing did not produce a single new job (net) in the U.S. economy. Instead, employment growth reflected activity primarily in the service sector (Bluestone and Harrison, 1987). This transition in the economic mix has the potential of lowering the standard of living and also increasing economic inequality by moving large proportions of middle-income households to lower income groups (Nelson and Lorence, 1988; Oregon Joint Legislative Committee on Trade and Economic Development, 1984; Sternlieb and Hughes, 1984:xi–xii).

In a case study of South Bend, Indiana, from 1956 to 1979, Peck and Shappell (1986) found that increasing employment in services occurring simultaneously with decreasing employment in manufacturing was associated with slower growth in wages across manufacturing and service industries. Apparently, the simultaneous decline in manufacturing depressed the local economy (Peck and Shappell, 1986). This could result in potential income multiplier effects from growth in services being inhibited.

Results from a study analyzing the effects of employment activity in various service, extraction, and manufacturing industries on median family income in 222 metropolitan areas substantiate distinctions between producer (export-oriented) and consumer service sectors. A large number of variables were controlled for, including earning differentials due to race, age, sex, and education, population size, regional location, and unemployment rate (Danziger, 1976). Employment in FIRE had a positive effect on the level of median income. A negative effect was found for wholesale/retail trade (Danziger, 1976), thereby substantiating the distinction between producer and consumer service sectors.[3] Bloomquist (1990:210) found using 1980 U.S. census data that employment in producer services leads to a greater range of employment opportunities for black men and women.

A more recent analysis of 130 Standard Metropolitan Statistical Areas (SMSAs) using 1980 data indicated that male employment activity in the service sector tended to depress median income levels, although the effect was not statistically significant for producer services.[4] Also, higher levels of male employment activity in the social and distributive services were associated with lower levels of income at the 5th and 95th percentiles. The same patterns were evident for female employment in the social and distributive services. In contrast, though, female employment in producer services was associated with significantly higher income levels for the 5th, 50th, and 95th percentiles (Nelson and Lorence, 1988: Table 2). In general, the effects of service sector employment on income levels were stronger for males than females (Nelson and Lorence, 1988: Table 2). Several variables were controlled for in this analysis, including population size, regional context, percentage black, percentage working full-time, and labor organizations activity (Nelson and Lorence, 1988).

Disagreement exists over the effect of growth in the sector on the distribution of income in the community. Although the earnings structure of the service sector tends to be bifurcated, there are some who suggest that increased reliance on service industries for employment, particularly those based on knowledge, such as education or research, will have an equalizing effect on income distributions as the work force becomes more homogeneous (Bell, 1973).

Also, Blau reasoned that growth in the service sector should promote the integration of groups in society (for example, racial groups), thereby implying that inequality should decrease. He expressed uncertainty over whether income differences would be reduced (Blau, 1980:19). However, recent evidence from case studies of several large retailing firms indicates that gender and racial barriers are being maintained. Stanback (1990) found that even though women comprise a large proportion of the retail work force, they are less likely to be found in higher-paying managerial positions. Also, there is considerable variability across firms regarding hiring practices of minorities, with some firms not hiring at lower or higher levels.

Nelson and Lorence's study, described above, on 130 SMSAs with 1980 data also analyzed the relationship between income inequality, using the Theil index, and male and female employment levels in the different service sectors. Higher levels of male employment in producer services were associated with higher levels of income inequality, while female employment in the social or distributive services was associated with higher levels of inequality (Nelson and Lorence, 1988: Table 2). The researchers, using the same model for 1970 data, found a positive association between the level of male employment activity in producer services and income inequality in metropolitan areas (Nelson and Lorence, 1985). Congruent with these findings, Tigges and Tootle (1990) found that employment in peripheral services resulted in increased part-time employment rather than full-time employment among men residing in urban areas.

On the other hand, Danziger's (1976) analysis of 222 SMSAs indicated that several producer service industries reduced income inequality, as measured by the Gini coefficient. Percentage employed in TCU (transportation, communications, and public utilities), professional and related services, and public administration were associated with reduced levels of inequality. The percentage employed in FIRE was also negatively related to inequality but missed reaching statistical significance ($t = 1.58$). In addition, the effects of durable and nondurable manufacturing were negative and significant (Danziger, 1976: Table 2).

The picture suggested by these studies is that the impact of change in economic structures on the level of income may be complex, since the shape of the composite earnings structure associated with rapidly growing service industries is bifurcated.

Other recent studies confirm that the relationship between changes in the distribution of income and the level of inequality is complex. A trend analysis of family incomes from 1969 to 1986 demonstrates that although the number of families in the middle income class declined, the proportion in the upper income class increased (Horrigan and Haugen, 1988). However, income inequality increased, since families in the lower income group received a decreasing share of aggregate income over the period studied. The increase in inequality occurred despite the size of the lower income group remaining relatively constant. Other research suggests that, overall, wages are decreasing and homogeneity in income levels is increasing, thereby leading to a reduction in income inequality. The drop in income levels reflects stagnation in both manufacturing and service sector wage rates (*Population Today*, 1988).[5]

INDUSTRIAL MIX AND THE DISTRIBUTION OF INCOME ACROSS PLACES

One aspect of the service sector appears certain: the various industries in the sector are associated with different wage rates. As noted above, consumer and retail services tend to have lower wage rates overall than industries classified as producer services (see Stanback and Noyelle, 1982: Table 3.3). A logical question to ask from the perspective of this research is whether both types of service sector firms will locate in smaller and more remote communities, or whether producer services will locate primarily in larger urban centers.

Several studies have considered the ability of service industries located in non-metropolitan areas to provide an export base for the local economy. However, they provide no direct evidence regarding the impact of service sector growth on community income levels and its distribution across places.

Studies from both the United Stattes and Great Britain indicate that higher-paying producer services tend to locate in more urbanized areas. In contrast, changes in consumer services are more evenly distributed across population size or region (Gillespie and Green, 1987; Hirschl and McReynolds, 1989; Miller and Bluestone, 1987:13–18). As a result, the beneficial effects of producer services on economic well-being may not occur extensively outside urbanized areas (Bloomquist, 1990). For smaller and more remote places, growth in the service sector represents primarily growth in the lower-wage consumer services, such as food service or auto repair and maintenance.

The economic transformation, or restructuring, involves moving from a dependence on manufacturing to one based upon the interdependence of production and service-producing industries. Consumer services, however, have played a small role in the transformation of the American economy (Noyelle and Stanback, 1983:16). If the participation of nonmetropolitan areas in the economic transformation is limited to a group of industries that play only a peripheral role in the process, the gap between metropolitan and nonmetropolitan places is expected to widen rather than narrow.

It appears that in some areas, and at least during the 1970s, low-wage manufacturing firms filtered down the urban hierarchy and into more remote and less populated centers (Moriarty, 1983). One possible reason for this filtering is that these firms were unable to compete with other firms paying higher wages for labor in urban centers. A related explanation is that the firms migrating to more remote areas possess "footlooseness" in terms of plant location, and so they migrate to areas with a reserve of labor, thereby enabling them to pay lower wages (Moriarty, 1983; Howes and Markusen, 1981).[6]

While the growth in services and manufacturing represents jobs, communities in more rural areas do not appear to be developing industrial structures typical of places displaying network prominence. Characteristics of network prominence are manufacturing activity in conjunction with the presence of advanced services (Ross, 1987). Service industries that are a component of the industrial structure for these places include distributive services, corporate activities, education, medical services, and the public sector (Noyelle, 1986a:150–54). All of these industries tend to be higher paying than the consumer services (Stanback and Noyelle, 1982:50).

Some research indicates that employment growth in the service sector in rural areas corresponds closely with growth in manufacturing and extractive industries. When growth in the goods-producing sector stopped after 1976, the service sector in rural areas also slowed considerably. In rural areas, then, development of the service sector, including the producer services, appears to be dependent on development of the goods-producing sector. Conversely, declines in goods production among metropolitan areas were not associated with declines in the growth rate for services; the service sector continued its expansion independent of the change in goods production (Bender, 1987; Miller and Bluestone, 1987:10–13). This suggests that rural areas cannot rely on service sector growth as a means of economic development, since employment growth is dependent on growth in the goods-producing sector.

However, other research contradicts these findings. Hirschl and McReynolds (1989) found that rural service sector growth has been concentrated in the social services, such as health care, education, and welfare, and that concentration in these industries was not related to employment in the goods-producing sector. Rather, economic activity in social services was related to the presence of income from non-work sources, such as that associated with the elderly (Hirschl and McReynolds, 1989). What is disconcerting is that the income potential of jobs in the social services tends to range from low to moderate. The earnings of about 50 percent of the workers in health and education are between 40 percent and 80 percent of the national average for all workers (Stanback and Noyelle, 1982: Table 3.3).[7]

Regardless of whether or not rural service sector growth is related to activity in the goods-producing sector, the tendency for producer services to localize in urban areas suggests that metropolitan dominance over hinterland areas, in terms of organizational control through employment structures, will continue as before (Ross, 1987; Frey, 1987).[8] What appears to be changing are the types of industries filtering down the hierarchy of settlements (Moriarty, 1983; Noyelle, 1986a; Frey, 1987; Ross, 1987). Rural areas are seeing an increase in manufacturing and services, but both appear to be low-wage-paying industries. Higher-paying firms tend to locate in centrally located places.

Evidence contradicting this interpretation exists, however. For example, a survey of businesses in nonmetropolitan counties revealed that, in general, there was no relationship between population size of the county where the business was located and percentage of the firm's sales made locally (Smith, 1984: Table 2, 3).[9] However, the level of exports does appear to be related to the remoteness of the firm's location. Export-oriented firms situated further from an SMSA or interstate highway had a lower percentage of sales exported from the county than more centrally located firms.

Although wages may be lower in service firms located in rural and noncentral urban areas, these firms can produce multiplier effects in local economies by bringing in nonlocal resources. In turn, these multiplier effects are expected to result in increased jobs and income due to reinvestment of these outside resources in the local economy (Smith, 1984:145–47; Smith and Pulver, 1978:13; 1981).

Since service sector industries have tended to comprise the high-growth economic sector, both during the 1970s and 1980s (Fuller and Gillis, 1986), service sector growth in rural communities can be beneficial for these localities. The diffusion of service sector firms to rural areas may indicate that these places are "catching up" with more urbanized localities in terms of the amount and variety of services offered (Smith, 1984:146). The view is taken that growth in the sector is viewed as a resource for local economic development.

However, even proponents of the service sector overlook the potential contribution of low-wage consumer services industries as a resource for the local economy (exceptions are Gillis, 1987:250–51; Marquand, 1979:34–35, 36). Places in economically depressed areas are the most likely to benefit from development of consumer service industries. Places undergoing economic decline or small communities with large proportions of elderly residents relying upon transfer payments from extralocal sources represent two examples of places likely to benefit from this low-wage sector.

Service industries such as fast-food restaurants can provide a basic contribution to the local economy since the money the firm receives is from extralocal sources (Gillis, 1987:250–51; Gruenstein and Guerra, 1981:22–23; Marquand, 1979:34–35, 36). Furthermore, firms serving residents in the locality result in these dollars being invested in the local economy rather than extralocally. This form of development is called import substitution, whereby local dollars are reinvested in the local economy. If these industries are also locally owned, dependencies on imported services (that is, provision of services by extralocal sources) are reduced (Gillis, 1987:251; Long, 1987:197–98; Marquand, 1979:35).

For instance, the presence of these consumer services increases the level of amenities associated with an area. These amenities are likely to help attract and retain residents who rely on transfer payments for income. Consumer services indirectly promote economic development by bringing extralocal dollars, in the form of transfer payments, into the community (Bender, 1987:70). Consistent with these findings, Tigges and Tootle (1990:348) found that service sector employment in peripheral industries reduces low-wage employment in rural areas.

COMPARING SERVICE AND MANUFACTURING INDUSTRIES

While various segments of the service sector are expected to help in sustaining and fueling the local economy, there is still concern over whether growth in services will make up for declines in manufacturing. If gains in the service sector are unable to compensate for income losses in manufacturing, community income levels will decline.

The literature reviewed in this section focuses on the negative aspects of manufacturing development, compared with development of the service sector. Some of this literature suggests that the location of the community in the urban hierarchy has a conditioning effect on the relationship between change in an industrial sector and income.

Concern has been expressed that the service sector will be unable to provide a basis for sustaining local and regional economies. An assumption underlying this belief is that jobs in the service sector contribute less to the basic or export economy than manufacturing or agriculture. However, questioning whether service sector firms are a desirable means for maintaining a stable economy ignores the issue of whether firms comprising the local economy in the past have been able to promote stability and well-being.

There is a considerable literature emphasizing the negative impact of absentee-owned industrial firms (for example, Pred, 1975; Barkley, 1978; Brue, 1975) and low-wage paying manufacturing firms (for example, Howes and Markusen, 1981). Thus, debate exists over the merits of manufacturing for improving social well-being, particularly low-wage and branch plant firms (Summers et al., 1976; Miller, 1980; Rogers et al., 1978). Several researchers maintain that the negative effects of growth in manufacturing tend to depress or inhibit potential benefits of the newly created jobs. Thus, the service sector may compare favorably with manufacturing if the negative effects of manufacturing and the positive effects of services have been underestimated.

In rural areas, dependence on absentee-controlled or low-wage manufacturing has been associated in some research with employment instability and lower incomes (McGranahan, 1982:35; Smith and Pulver, 1978). Also, local multiplier effects from rural manufacturing developments have tended to be overestimated (Summers et al., 1976:4). In addition, a capital-intensive export base, such as one relying on manufacturing or extractive industries, may be poorly articulated with the local economy. Not only may multipliers be less than expected, but these export industries may induce a decline in the local economy. Benefits from manufacturing growth may accrue to only a few, thereby leading to a decline in income levels and increased inequality (Long, 1987; Moore, 1980). Moreover, many manufacturing plants place heavy demands on community infrastructures. Service firms, on the other hand, do not place as many demands on local infrastructure (Smith and Pulver, 1978).

The differential impacts of the service and manufacturing sectors on community income may depend upon the location of the community in the urban hierarchy. Some researchers have argued that the types of service firms locating in core metropolitan areas, such as New York City, Chicago, or Los Angeles, are often headquarters of multilocational firms. Also, firms associated with the goods production process, such as advertising, are found in these places. As stated before, these industries tend to be high-paying (Noyelle, 1986a; Noyelle and Stanback; 1983; Stanback and Noyelle, 1982). For example, the 1974 average annual wage for export-oriented service industries (including contract construction) was $10,160, while for manufacturing the average was $10,503 (Smith and Pulver, 1981:37–38). Thus, earning differences between export-oriented services and manufacturing appear to be small, at least on average.

For smaller and more remote communities, growth in services (and manufacturing) may represent a new source of jobs, albeit low-wage ones (Summers et al., 1976:2–4). These jobs would represent a boon if preexisting jobs are typically low-wage and there are an insufficient number of year-round jobs for the local population. However, whether income benefits from manufacturing exceed or fall below those of the service sector remains an empirical question.

CONCLUSIONS

Because of the dearth of data reporting economic activity in the service sector, there have been few empirical investigations seeking to substantiate or discredit assumptions about the effects of growth in services (Long, 1987:200; Riddle, 1986:4). The shortage of good data on services is perpetuated by characteristics common to service firms. Diversity in the types of firms called services, their products, the processes involved in producing the service, and the classification schemes used to describe the service sector contribute to the difficulties involved in locating and gathering information on service industries (Marshall, 1988:5; Menchik, 1981:237). Compounding these problems are the smallness of firm size, high failure rates of new businesses, and the low level of capital necessary to start up a business (Menchik, 1981:237, 244).

In the next chapter, the sample and model used in the analysis of Mid-Atlantic community data from the 1970s are described. Empirical results for this sample are discussed in the fourth chapter. The goal of this analysis, as well as the analysis of county-level data for the entire United States in the fifth chapter, is to fill some of the gaps in the empirical literature surrounding this issue area.

NOTES

1. Stanback and Noyelle (1982) list these figures for 1975; they are taken from the U.S. Bureau of the Census, Survey of Income and Education, 1976. The U.S. average earnings were $8,610 in 1975.

2. These data also are for 1975 and from Survey of Income and Education, 1976, published by the U.S. Bureau of the Census.

3. The strength of the effect for wholesale/retail trade may be confounded or weakened, since the trend analysis presented earlier indicates that wholesale and retail trade have opposite effects on income levels. Generally, retail trade is classified as a low-wage consumer service, and wholesale trade is typed as a distributive service, which has a medium- to high-wage scale (Stanback and Noyelle, 1982:8–9).

Also, results from Danziger's analysis should be interpreted cautiously. It is likely that the results are affected by multicollinearity due to the inclusion of all industry categories in the equation except the residual category, "Industry not reported" (Danziger, 1976:469: Table 2). The sum of percentage employed for all industries in the regression equation is probably close to one for many cases. In congruence with this assessment, the regression coefficients tended not to reach statistical significance at the 0.05 level and often the 0.10 level (Danziger, 1976: Table 2). Multicollinearity produces instability among the regression coefficients, meaning the values of the coefficients are highly dependent on the particular data set. Signs of regression coefficients can flip for affected variables. This instability is reflected in large standard errors for affected coefficients, and hence, low t-values (Myers, 1986:75–86).

4. Occupation, rather than industry employment, was used to measure service sector activity. Examples of producer services activities are financial activities, accounting, and other business services; personal services included entertainment, repairs, eating and drinking; and social services encompassed professional services such as education, medi-

cine, and government. Distributive services included both wholesale and retail trade (Nelson and Lorence, 1988:499). As in Danziger's analysis, the effect for wholesale/retail trade may be misleading since separate effects were not estimated for each industry.

5. These two studies exemplify the lack of consistency among trend analyses of income. Factors that appear to be important for obtaining consistent results are the methods for delineating the lower, middle, and upper income groups, and whether the years being compared are similar in terms of being a peak or trough in the business cycle. It should be noted that the two years compared in this study, 1969 and 1979, are comparable, since both are peak years (Horrigan and Haugen, 1988; McMahon and Tschetter, 1986; Rosenthal, 1985).

6. However, there is evidence that some nonmetropolitan areas in the South were attracting higher-wage and less labor-intensive industries than expected, although they were not as high-wage or capital-intensive as other firms in the South or United States as a whole (Till, 1974:19).

7. These data also are for 1975 and from Survey of Income and Education, 1976, published by the U.S. Bureau of the Census.

8. Deviations from traditional network arrangements of cities may occur due to the increased importance of certain types of industries in the service sector, such as corporate (Noyelle, 1986a) or government (Ross, 1987) activities, resulting in a reordering of some cities in terms of network prominence. However, those cities most central in the network, termed "command and control centers" (Noyelle, 1986a), are expected to remain dominant. It is the lower-order centers, characterized by a heavy dependence on declining manufacturing sectors, which may not retain the prominence they held during the 1970s (Noyelle, 1986a).

9. The sample consisted of nonmanufacturing firms located in nonmetropolitan counties (Smith, 1984:149–52).

3

Sampling Design and Model Specification

The relationship between increasing service sector employment and changes in income is examined in two separate analyses with different time frames. The first and most detailed analysis, which is discussed in this chapter and the fourth, examines changes in the economic structure of communities in the Mid-Atlantic region (New Jersey, New York, and Pennsylvania) during the 1970s. The second analysis, which is discussed in the fifth chapter, is based on county-level data. However, relative to the first analysis, only limited data is available for the second analysis.[1]

This chapter describes and justifies, in terms of demographic trends, the sample and time frame used in the Mid-Atlantic analysis. Variables in the model used to assess the impact of changes in the employment structure on income and its distribution are also specified. The effects of changing employment activity in the manufacturing and service sectors of the local economy are of primary interest. Dependent variables measure social well-being in terms of income structures at the community level.

The sample consists of 642 communities in the Mid-Atlantic region of the country. All communities in the states of New Jersey, New York, and Pennsylvania (except New York City and Philadelphia) are included. Communities were created by aggregating geographically contiguous minor civil divisions (MCDs), and are intended to represent places where residents are functionally interdependent. Appendix A provides a technical discussion of the conceptual definition of community and the method used to operationalize the concept.

THE MID-ATLANTIC REGION

Because transition from a manufacturing-based to a service-based economy occurred with great clarity in the Mid-Atlantic region during the 1970s, this region was chosen as the site for studying the effects of industrial transition. Also, the large proportion of communities in the region in rural areas lets one examine whether movement toward a service-based economy has different implications for social well-being among rural and urban places.

Demographic trends indicate that the northeastern United States, and in particular, the Mid-Atlantic region, is undergoing a transition from dependency on manufacturing to services as a source of jobs and wages. Although nearly 1.5 million manufacturing jobs were created in the United States from 1960 to 1975, the Northeast lost 781,000 jobs. The bulk of these losses occurred in the Mid-Atlantic states (Sternlieb and Hughes, 1978:9).

The Mid-Atlantic region lost jobs in manufacturing at a faster rate than the United States as a whole (Fuller, 1986:v, 6). While the Mid-Atlantic states had a heavier dependence on manufacturing employment than the United States during the first half of the 1970s, they had less than the national average employed in manufacturing by 1984 (Fuller, 1986:v).

In general, major metropolitan centers tended to lose jobs in the goods-producing sector (Noyelle and Stanback, 1983:2). New York City and Philadelphia contributed strongly to the decline in the region, with both cities losing about 30 percent of the total number of manufacturing jobs lost in 1970 (Sternlieb and Hughes, 1978:9). Most losses in the goods-producing sector occurred during the 1970–1975 period.

However, 90 percent of the 19 million jobs created in the United States as a whole during the 1970s were in the service sector. Major cities of the Mid-Atlantic, while losing jobs in manufacturing, were pulling in service sector jobs by attracting administrative offices in the private, public, and nonprofit sectors, as well as distributive service industries (Noyelle, 1986a:151). For instance, the Mid-Atlantic region had a higher proportion of its total employment in the service sector than the United States did during the 1974–1984. Furthermore, the rate of employment growth in the service sector in the Mid-Atlantic region increased during the 1974–1984 period (Fuller, 1986:2–3, Table 2, 3).[2] Thus during the 1970s, the Mid-Atlantic states underwent a transition from dependency on the goods-producing sector to dependency on the service sector.

COMPARING THE MID-ATLANTIC WITH OTHER REGIONS

The Mid-Atlantic region had the lowest employment growth rate of any region in the United States during the 1970s. Also, it was the only region which experienced a decline in that growth rate over the prior decade (Fuller, 1982:6–7).

Employment growth rates for the 1962–71 period and the 1971–78 period for various regions in the United States are graphed in Figure 3.1. Each region's share

Figure 3.1
Annual Employment Growth Rates

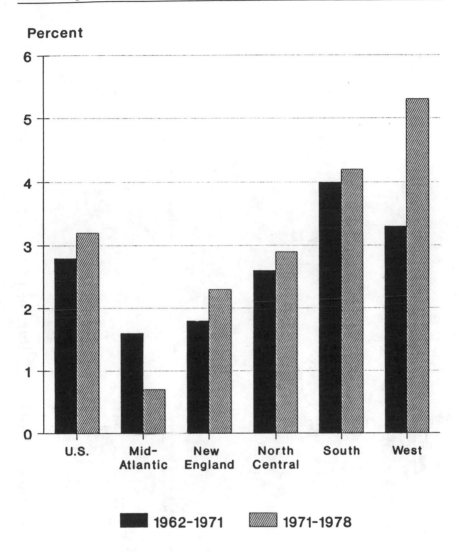

Source: Data from Fuller, 1982

of total employment in the United States in 1962 and 1978 are pictured in Figure 3.2a.

In the western region of the United States, the employment growth rate went from 3.3 percent during the 1960s to 5.3 percent in the 1970s; the share of em-

Figure 3.2
Regional Shares of Employment, 1962 and 1978

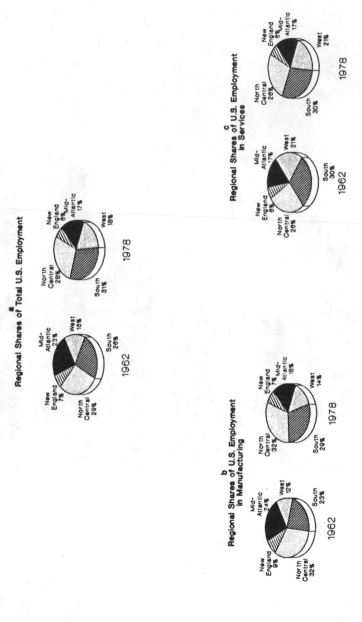

a
Regional Shares of Total U.S. Employment

New England 7%
Mid-Atlantic 23%
West 15%
North Central 29%
South 26%

1962

New England 6%
Mid-Atlantic 17%
West 18%
North Central 28%
South 31%

1978

b
Regional Shares of U.S. Employment in Manufacturing

New England 9%
Mid-Atlantic 24%
West 12%
North Central 32%
South 23%

1962

New England 7%
Mid-Atlantic 18%
West 14%
North Central 32%
South 29%

1978

c
Regional Shares of U.S. Employment in Services

New England 6%
Mid-Atlantic 17%
West 21%
North Central 26%
South 30%

1962

New England 6%
Mid-Atlantic 17%
West 21%
North Central 26%
South 30%

1978

Source: Data from Fuller, 1982; U.S. Bureau of the Census, 1963; 1979

ployment going to the West also increased from 15.3 percent to 18.3 percent. The South and north central regions both experienced small gains during the 1970s in their respective employment growth rates over the prior decade. However, while the north central region underwent a small decline in its share of employment, the South experienced a considerable increase from 25.7 percent of total U.S. employment in 1962 to 30.6 percent in 1978 (Fuller, 1982: Figures 2 and 4).

While the Mid-Atlantic and New England regions had similar employment growth rates during the 1960s of about 1.6 percent, their respective employment trends diverged during the 1970s. The employment growth rate increased to 2.3 percent in New England, while in the Mid-Atlantic it declined considerably to 0.7 percent (Fuller, 1982:7). Each region also saw a decline in its share of total U.S. employment.

Each region's share of total employment in the United States corresponds roughly with its proportion of manufacturing employment. While the Mid-Atlantic experienced a large decline in its share of manufacturing employment between 1962 and 1978 (from 24 percent to 18 percent), the South and West experienced gains comparable to that experienced in total employment. Also similar to the patterns in total employment, the north central region experienced only minor change in its share of manufacturing employment (Fuller, 1982:10–12; U.S. Bureau of the Census, 1963: Table 297; 1979: Table 680). Figure 3.2b depicts change in each region's share of manufacturing employment between 1962 and 1978.

Changes in the each region's share of employment in services also reflect trends occurring in manufacturing and the employment shift to southern and western regions of the United States. Between 1962 and 1978, the Mid-Atlantic's share of services employment declined from 22 percent to 17 percent, although New England saw only a minor decline (7 percent to 6 percent). Also, the north central region lost some of its share by declining from 28 percent to 26 percent. On the other hand, the South and West increased their share of service employment; the South went from 26 percent in 1962 to 30 percent in 1978, while the West went from 17 percent to 20 percent (U.S. Bureau of the Census, 1963: Table 297; 1979: Table 680). Figure 3.2c portrays these trends.

Associated with such changes in the structure of employment, and the redistribution of jobs across the United States, both New England and the Mid-Atlantic experienced a decline in per capita income as a percentage of the U.S. per capita income. Adjusting for differences in cost of living, per capita income in New England fell from 96 percent of the U.S. average in 1970 to 89 percent in 1975. The Mid-Atlantic region also saw a decline from 104 percent to 100 percent. Conversely, per capita income in the southwestern and Plains states increased from 96 percent of the U.S. average in 1970 to 99 percent in 1975, and in the Rocky Mountain states it went from 93 percent to 98 percent of the U.S. average (ACIR, 1980: Table 2).

The transition to a service-based economy from manufacturing, in the short term, appears to have made the regions more similar as per capita income and dependence on manufacturing became more evenly distributed. However, the transition from dependence on manufacturing apparently created hardship among workers and families in the Mid-Atlantic region during the 1970s. Due to the depressed economy, the capacity of the service sector to generate income could be inhibited. By using the Mid-Atlantic region as the sample, estimates of the effects of service sector growth may, therefore, have a more conservative or negative bias. This allows us to examine, under a worst-case scenario, the short-term effects on income and its distribution when the service sector is substituted for lost jobs in manufacturing.

RURAL AND URBAN COMMUNITIES IN THE MID-ATLANTIC REGION

Another consideration in selecting the sample for the study is whether communities exhibit sufficient variability in terms of population size. Because remoteness of a place is expected to condition the effect of changes in industrial mix on community income levels, it is necessary for the sample to include sufficiently large proportions of rural and urban places. The Mid-Atlantic region has a relatively large segment of the population classified as rural. Pennsylvania had the largest rural population in the United States in the 1970 and 1980 censuses. New York was ranked fourth in 1970 and sixth in 1980 in number of rural inhabitants. In contrast, New Jersey is heavily urbanized; it was ranked 29th and 30th in 1960 and 1970, respectively (U.S. Bureau of the Census, 1983: Table 16).

Also, a large number of places were classified as rural in both Pennsylvania and New York in the 1970 Census; 634 (54 percent) and 402 (46 percent) of places had a population of 2,500 or less in Pennsylvania and New York, respectively. Again, the higher level of urbanization in New Jersey is reflected in the relatively smaller number of rural places in the state; 70 (18 percent) had a population of 2,500 or less (U.S. Bureau of the Census, 1973: Table 19). These numbers remained fairly constant over the 1970–80 decade (U.S. Bureau of the Census, 1983: Table 14).[3]

Considerable variability exists among communities in the sample with respect to rurality: population size among communities in the sample used in this study ranges from 1,145 to 806,891, while the distance of communities from an interstate highway, a measure of remoteness, ranges from zero to 96 miles. The results presented above lend additional support for the decision to designate the Mid-Atlantic states as the sample from which to test the research hypotheses.

TIME SPAN: 1970 TO 1980

The 1970 to 1980 time span represents an appropriate period for studying the impact of increasing service employment on social well-being. During the 1970s and early 1980s, major structural changes occurred in domestic and international economic activities (Noyelle, 1986b:10–11). These structural changes include increased economic activity in services, the mass-scale introduction of computerized technology, the increased importance of small firms in generating new jobs, and increased international competition for manufacturing and service sector jobs (Noyelle, 1986b:10–13).

In conjunction with the population turnaround, manufacturing firms during this decade shifted locations among regions, while at the same time shifting to more rural locations (Sternlieb and Hughes, 1978:15). Employment in manufacturing decreased in metropolitan areas and increased in rural areas over the 1970–80 decade. In the Mid-Atlantic states, metropolitan areas followed this national trend, while nonmetropolitan areas in this region tended to follow an attenuated form of the national trend. About 33 percent of nonmetropolitan places in the Mid-Atlantic states experienced a decline in manufacturing employment during the 1970s, as compared to 45 percent in the 1960s (Fuller, 1982:29).

The growing dominance of the service sector as a source of employment has been transforming the structure of the economy. Both rural and urban areas in the United States as a whole experienced increases in service employment during the 1970–1980 period (Miller and Bluestone, 1987:11; Noyelle and Stanback, 1983:16; Pulver, 1986c:3).

A caveat to this generalization is that there are differences in the types of service firms locating in metropolitan and nonmetropolitan areas. While metropolitan centers experienced increases in nonprofit, government, and production-related services (Noyelle and Stanback, 1983:14), rural areas mainly experienced increases in consumer-related services and export-oriented services related to extractive industries (Miller and Bluestone, 1987:15). However, as noted in the first chapter, consumer-related services constitute only a small role in the transformation of the American economy (Noyelle and Stanback, 1983:16). In addition, consumer-related firms are characterized as providing low-wage work (Oregon Joint Legislative Committee on Trade and Economic Development, 1984:10; Stanback and Noyelle, 1982).

If the extent to which nonmetropolitan areas participate in the economic transformation is limited to a group of service industries that play only a peripheral role in the process, then the gap between metropolitan and nonmetropolitan America is expected to widen rather than narrow. The rural/urban turnaround of the 1970s would result in the solidification of the hierarchy of places, with rurality of residence becoming increasingly indicative of limited job and income opportunities.

SOURCES OF DATA

Secondary data are used for the analysis, and all variables are measured at two points in time. The U.S. Census of Population for 1970 and 1980 on minor civil divisions (MCDs) are used to provide information on aggregate income and its distribution in these communities. This information is reported for 1969 and 1979, respectively, in the two censuses. In order to obtain community-level estimates of income, MCD-level data was aggregated within each community in a manner described in Appendix A.

Data on the types of firms and number of employees present in localities are from Dun and Bradstreet's Marketing Identifiers file. The firm-level data from this file were aggregated to the community level. Available data, however, are for the years 1969 and 1978. The one-year difference between the census data and Dun and Bradstreet is a potential threat to the internal validity of the design (Campbell and Stanley, 1963), though probably not a substantial one. It seems likely that changes occurring in the level and distribution of resources during the one-year interval between 1978 and 1979 would not be enough to affect the relationship between changing industrialization patterns and the level and distribution of resources. Appendix B discusses measurement issues in using Dun and Bradstreet data files.

MEASURES OF CONCEPTS

The model presented in this chapter is designed to assess the impact of industrial transition on change in social well-being. Social well-being refers to the level of resources in the community and the distribution of those resources. While the United States census presents data on income for families and unrelated individuals, only family income will be used to measure community resources.[4]

Change in social well-being is measured by three separate concepts: (1) change in community aggregate income, (2) change in the distribution of income across the community, and (3) change in the distribution of income across communities in the Mid-Atlantic. Industrial transition is defined as the difference in the number employed by an industrial sector over the two periods. The major independent variables in the model are changes in the number employed in various types of manufacturing and service industries. In short, the model examines the effect of changing employment in various industries on change in community income, and the distribution of income within communities, as well as between rural and urban places.

Measuring the Level and Distribution of Income

Aggregate family income in the community is used to measure the level of resources available in the local economy. Change in aggregate income is defined as the difference in aggregate family income between 1979 and 1969 (in 1982 constant, or inflation-adjusted, dollars[5]).

Differences in the number of families in the various income groups (these being the lower, middle, upper, and highest income brackets), between 1969 and 1979 are used to measure change in the distribution of income in the community. Data on the income distribution is grouped since it is from the U.S. Census of Population summary data files for MCDs.[6] Table 3.1 presents the lower and upper bounds in 1982 constant dollars for the lower, middle, upper, and highest income groups.[7]

Table 3.1
Lower and Upper Bounds on Comparable Income Categories for the 1970 and 1980 U.S. Census

Income Categories	Lower	1969 to	Upper	Lower	to	1979 Upper
Lower	$0		$13,165	$0		$13,290
Lowest	$0		$10,532	$0		$9968
Upper Lower	$10,532		$13,165	$9968		$13,290
Middle	$13,165		$39,459	$13,290		$39,870
Lower Middle	$13,165		$26,330	$13,290		$26,580
Upper Middle	$26,330		$39,495	$26,580		$39,870
Upper	$39,495		$65,825	$39,870		$66,450
Highest	$65,825+			$66,450+		

The objective in analyzing the second measure of social well-being, distribution of income in the community, is to determine if the service sector is inducing bifurcation in income structure. Greater bifurcation implies that income inequality is increasing. As discussed in the second chapter, much research literature suggests that a transition to service-producing industries will result in the transfer of workers from the middle to lower income groups.

The third measure of social well-being focuses on change in the distribution of income across communities. Communities are ranked with respect to the proportion of aggregate family income each one contributed to the total for the Mid-Atlantic region for 1969 and 1979.[8] The difference in ranked position with respect to the community's share of total income in the region over the decade indicates the shift in the share of community's resources over the decade, thereby measuring the extent to which income is redistributed across communities in the region. The difference in rank is analyzed in order to see how changes in industrial mix influence change in the position of the community in the hierarchy, based upon aggregate income.

Measuring the Community's Industrial Mix

Of particular interest is the impact of industrial transition on the availability of resources, especially at the lower end of the income distribution. The classification scheme used in this study distinguishes firms offering low-wage work from those offering higher wages.

The two-digit 1972 Standard Industrial Classification (SIC) code reported on firms in the Dun and Bradstreet Reference Book Listings is used to classify firms into four categories: (1) high-wage service firms, (2) low-wage service firms, (3) low-wage manufacturing firms, and (4) high-wage manufacturing firms. Low-wage and high-wage industry categories are treated as mutually exclusive and exhaustive categories. The classification of manufacturing firms as low- or high-wage-paying is based on average weekly earnings for two-digit 1972 SIC manufacturing industries in the Mid-Atlantic states, reported by the U.S. Department of Labor (1979).[9]

The following manufacturing industries are classified as low-wage: tobacco, textile mill products, apparel, lumber products and furniture, rubber products, leather products, and miscellaneous manufacturing industries. All other manufacturing industries are classified as high-wage.[10] Examples of industries in the high-wage manufacturing category include transportation equipment, primary metal, printing, and food products. Differences between the low- and high-wage groups are fairly clear-cut: average weekly earnings for all but one of the low-wage industries listed across the three states is below $210/week, while the lowest average weekly earnings for high-wage manufacturing is $232/week.

Service industries are dichotomized also into low-wage- and high-wage-paying firms. High-wage service firms tend to function in conjunction with the provision of goods, such as payment plans or warranty plans, or are incorporated within the goods-production process, such as advertising or customizing (Noyelle, 1986a:146). Lower-wage retail and consumer service firms tend to be less specialized and more freestanding; they provide services for meeting consumer needs rather than complementing the goods-production work process (Noyelle, 1986a; Miller and Bluestone, 1987). Retail and consumer services include retail stores, personal services, auto repair, and recreation. Producer, distributive, and non-profit services are classified as high-wage service industries; included within this group are finance, insurance, real estate (FIRE), business services, transportation, health, and education services.[11] Table 3.2 lists the two-digit SIC groups included in each of the manufacturing and service industry categories.

Government and government enterprises (that is, public administration) are excluded from the analyses. Coverage on these agencies by Dun and Bradstreet tends to be poor since they rarely have need for a credit report (Birch, 1979:5–7). Also, nonmanufacturing and nonservice industries are excluded from analyses; these include, for example, agriculture, mining, and construction. Excluding this group of firms, along with government enterprises, reduces problems associated with multicollinearity in the regression analyses.

It is likely that there is a great deal of variety within categories of industries, such as textiles and retail services (Howes and Markusen, 1981:456). Hence, this classification scheme reflects only general tendencies for types of firms to have the same configuration of wage levels.

Table 3.2
Classification of Service and Manufacturing Industries into Low-wage and High-wage Sectors

SERVICE INDUSTRIES:

Low-Wage (SIC code)
Retail trade	(52-59)
Hotels	(70)
Personal services	(72)
Auto repair	(75)
Misc. repair services	(76)
Motion pictures	(78)
Amusement & recreation	(79, 84)
Private households	(88)

High-Wage (SIC code)
Transportation, communication & util.	(40-49)
Finance, insurance & real estate	(60-67)
Business services	(73)
Legal services	(81)
Membership organizations	(86)
Misc. professional serv.	(89)
Social services	(83)
Health services	(80)
Educational services	(82)

MANUFACTURING INDUSTRIES:

Low-Wage (SIC code)
Tobacco manufactures	(21)
Textile mill products	(22)
Apparel	(23)
Lumber products, incl. furniture & fixtures	(24, 25)
Rubber products	(30)
Leather products	(31)
Misc. manufacturing indus.	(39)

High-Wage (SIC code)
Food and kindred products	(20)
Paper, printing, publishing and allied products	(26, 27)
Chemicals, petroleum refining, related & allied indus.	(28, 29)
Stone, clay, glass, & concrete products	(32)
Primary metal industries	(33)
Fabricated metal products, machinery, electrical & electronic	(34-36)
Transportation equipment	(37)
Measuring, analyzing & controlling instruments	(38)

Table 3.2 continued
_____

```
EXCLUDED INDUSTRIES:

     Government, justice, finance,
       administration of public
       programs, & national
       security                          (91-97)
     Agriculture, forestry,
       & fishing                         (01-09)
     Mining                              (10-14)
     Construction                        (15-17)
```

The decision to use firms rather than occupations as the basis for measuring transition in the economic structure of the local society is consistent with the research question. Interest is on the impact of industrial structure on social well-being, and industrial structure is defined by the types of firms present in the locale. The industrial structure of a place is viewed as a constraining force on well-being, since most people take jobs that are created by firms. Measuring changes in the occupational structure of the locality is more reflective of questions dealing with changes in bureaucratization of the economy, since the number of service occupations can increase in goods-producing firms, but the wage levels of the same occupation often differ by industry. For example, managers in the retail and consumer service industries tend to be paid less than managers in other service industries (Stanback and Noyelle, 1982:33, Table 3.2).

SPECIFYING THE MODEL

The following section presents the model used to estimate the effect of the changing structure of employment in services and manufacturing on community income between 1969 and 1979.

In order to determine the impact of the service sector on aggregate income, relative to the effect of manufacturing, differences in the number employed in low- and high-wage service and manufacturing firms between 1970 and 1978 are calculated and included in the model. Since the prior level of dependence on a sector is likely to affect the amount of subsequent growth (or decline) in that sector (Perry, 1980; Stanback and Noyelle, 1982), the number employed in a given sector for 1970 also is included in the model.

In addition, the preexisting structure of the local economy is expected to affect the impact of change in a sector on the level and distribution of resources in a local economy. For example, a loss of manufacturing jobs in a community with an economy built around manufacturing would result in the local economy being in a weaker position than a loss of manufacturing jobs in a community not as dependent on that sector. Interactions between the level of dependency on a sector and subsequent growth in that sector are therefore included in the model.[12]

Compared with urban areas, rural areas in the Mid-Atlantic states are more dependent on declining economic sectors such as manufacturing (Brown and Deavers, 1987:3–5; Fuller, 1986:7–11). Growth of the service sector in rural areas would lessen this dependency. Consequently, services, including the low-wage consumer service sector, are expected to have a more beneficial impact on remote places than centrally located ones, because the existing economic base in rural areas is not as stable. Hence, interactions between remoteness of a place and the growth in low-wage and high-wage service sectors are included in the model.

The local economy of the community is characterized as being service-based, diversified, dependent on high-wage manufacturing, or dependent on low-wage manufacturing. These categories were developed in order to summarize the composition of the industrial mix of the community; they are based on a cluster analysis of the different industry variables. Refer to Appendix E for a description of the procedures used in the cluster analysis to develop this classification scheme and a summary of the results.

Several control variables are included in the analysis. As mentioned before, preexisting levels of resources are expected to affect the amount of change occurring in those resources (Perry, 1980). To control for the initial level of aggregate resources in the community, population size and its quadratic effect are included. The quadratic effect is included in order to measure the extent to which the largest places may have experienced declines in aggregate resources (Fuguitt, 1985:260), in contrast to the positive relationship that may have existed between population size and aggregate income for smaller and more moderately sized places.

It may be noted that aggregate community income and the number of families in each income group in 1969 are highly correlated with population size. The Pearson correlation coefficient between 1970 population size and 1969 aggregate income is 0.97; the correlation coefficient is 0.91, 0.99, 0.94, and 0.81, respectively, with the number of families in 1969 in the lower, middle, upper, and highest income groups.[13] Therefore, initial population size serves as a proxy variable for the initial level of community aggregate income and income distribution in the regressions, where the dependent variable is either change in aggregate income or change in income distribution. When change in the rank position of the community in the income hierarchy is the dependent variable, the rank of the community in 1969 is included, since the correlation of population size with this covariate is considerably smaller ($r = 0.56$), though statistically significant at the 0.001 level.

Change in the community's population size between 1970 and 1980 controls on corresponding change in aggregate income and in the number of families falling into each of the different income groups. In order to model the process of population change and the corresponding change in aggregate resources accurately, an interaction between initial population size of a place and change in population over the decade is included. This term reflects the observed tendency of smaller places to increase in size while metropolitan centers experienced declines during the 1970s (see, for example, Fuguitt, 1985).

Also included as a measure of resources is the median value of a home in the community. This variable indicates the standard (and cost) of living associated with residing in a particular community. Percentage of employees employed by headquarters (HQ) firms in the surrounding multicounty labor market area is included in order to measure the extent to which bureaucratic control of industries is vested in the surrounding region.[14] Company headquarters tend to buy more of their inputs within the region than branch plants, while branch plants tend to buy inputs through the parent company (Marquand, 1979:35). Hence, a predominance of headquarters firms in a region would indicate a flow of extra-locally generated resources into the community. Also, import substitution would occur when headquarters firms purchase inputs locally.

Communities with higher proportions of groups experiencing discrimination in terms of hiring and wage levels are expected to have lower aggregate incomes as well as higher proportions of families in the lower end of the income distribution. The percentage of females in the work force in 1970 and percentage change between 1970 and 1980 are entered as control variables. Similarly, the percentage of minorities in the population and percentage change between 1970 and 1980 are included. Increases in service sector employment are associated with greater participation of females in the work force, although the jobs tend to be lower paying (Browne, 1986:23–24; Stanback and Noyelle, 1982:40; Urquhart, 1984:20).

Also, the 1970 percentage of the population that is elderly and the 1970–80 percentage change in this group are entered, since the elderly can constitute an economic resource for the community by bringing in extralocal income in the form of transfer payments (see Gillis, 1987; Li and MacLean, 1989). Furthermore, rural areas generally have larger proportions of elderly in the population (Johansen and Fuguitt, 1984).

For the most part, the results in the fourth chapter can be interpreted easily. When the dependent variable is change in the number of families in a certain income group, regression coefficients indicate the effect of a new job in a particular industrial sector, such as low-wage services, on the number of families in, say, the middle income group. The effects of each industrial sector can be mapped across the different income groups; the result is a statement about the effect of that sector on the community income distribution.

When the dependent variable is change in community aggregate income, regression coefficients indicate the change in community income associated with an increase of a single job in a particular industrial sector. In other words, the regression coefficients indicate the worth of a job in dollars to the community, for example, in high-wage services. And, when the dependent variable is change in the position of the community in the income hierarchy, the regression coefficients indicate the effect of a gain of one job in a particular sector on the gain (or loss) of position in the hierarchy.

Table 3.3
Descriptive Statistics for Variables in Model: Mid-Atlantic Sample

Variables:	Mean	Median	Std. Dev.	Minimum Value	Maximum Value
DEPENDENT:					
Change in Aggregate Family Income (1979-1969) (in $100,000)	229.08	133.22	1093.57	-12236.1	10630.0
Distribution of Income Within Community					
Change in Number of Families (1979-1969)					
Lower Income Class	284	96	742	-1216	7963
Middle Income Class	-192	68	2263	-27693	16764
Upper Income Class	322	134	799	-4827	8036
Highest Income Class	92	22	352	-3830	2419
Change in Half-Share Coefficient (1979-1969)	0.32	1.79	11.18	-35.0	31.1
Change in Variance of the Logarithms (1979-1969)	0.03	0.04	0.06	-0.19	0.23
Change in Position of Community in Income Hierarchy (1979-1969)	0	-1	30	-102	203
INDEPENDENT:					
Population Size (1970) (in 1,000)	39.31	11.63	84.03	1.14	806.89
Change in Population Size (1980-1970) (in 1,000)	0.51	0.58	11.06	-125.33	120.87
Population Size in 1970 x Amount of Change in Population Quadratic Effect: (Population Size for 1970)					
Number of Employees (1970)					
High-Wage Manufacturing	3761	618	9994	0	104409
High-Wage Services	1372	182	4902	0	69424
Low-Wage Manufacturing	915	152	2482	0	24217
Low-Wage Services	1365	316	3559	1	42025
Change in Number of Employees (1978-1970)					
High-Wage Manufacturing	-844	-4	4363	-49235	9585
High-Wage Services	1239	184	3631	-21748	47038
Low-Wage Manufacturing	-202	-5	1128	-12698	7428
Low-Wage Services	368	86	1708	-11356	3197
Number of Employees in 1970 x Amount of Change in					
Low-Wage Manufacturing	-2290376	-69	1.8E-7	-3.1E-8	5.1E-7
Low-Wage Services	1060901	19164	1.7E-7	-2.1E-8	2.6E-8
Distance to Interstate Highway	16	10	17	0	96
Distance from Highway x Amount of Change in					
High-Wage Services	8419	896	26862	-138368	358088
Low-Wage Services	3403	565	13669	-87804	155142

Table 3.3 continued

Independent Variables (cont.):	Mean	Median	Std. Dev.	Minimum Value	Maximum Value
Industrial Mix Categories (1970)[a]					
Service-based	0.36	--	0.48	--	--
Based on High-Wage Manufacturing					
	0.22	--	0.42	--	--
Based on Low-Wage Manufacturing					
	0.07	--	0.26	--	--
Diversified	0.34	--	0.47	--	--
Median Value of Home (in $1000)	41	38	17	10	135
Percentage of Employees in HQ Firms in Labor Market Area (1970)					
	16.0	16.9	6.5	2.3	31.5
Percentage in 1970					
Females in Work Force	36.1	36.2	3.8	15.3	51.8
Minority Population	2.8	0.8	5.0	0	49.4
Elderly Population	10.7	10.6	3.0	3.2	29.6
Percentage Change Between 1980 and 1970					
Females in Work Force	40.5	33.7	32.2	-28.2	307.8
Minority Population	150.4	57.2	329.4	-100.0	4900.0
Elderly Population	26.8	23.1	25.1	-28.9	404.8

a. These figures are based on a set of four dummy variables, each coded zero and one, with one indicating the community is characterized by that industrial mix. The mean of a dummy variable is equivalent to the proportion of the sample with that mix, the standard deviation is a measure of dispersion. The median and minimum and maximum values provide no additional information.

Preliminary analyses indicate that including one of the dummy variables in the equation is sufficient since industry effects are modeled extensively with the variables listed above.

Since the units of all industrial sector variables are the same (that is, the number of employees in a sector), the regression coefficients are comparable to each other. This means the effects of low-wage and high-wage service sectors can be compared with corresponding sectors in manufacturing.

The model for estimating the impact of service sector growth is modified slightly for each of the dependent variables. Nonsignificant interaction terms involving industrial change variables are deleted when appropriate in order to obtain more precise estimates of the effects of service and manufacturing sector employment on the income distribution. However, terms containing population size and change always remained in the model in order to ensure adequate controls on these variables.

Descriptive statistics for variables in the model are presented in Table 3.3. Means, standard deviations, and nonparametric (that is, robust) statistics are pro-

Table 3.4
Percentiles for Industry and Population Variables

Variables:	1%	10%	25%	75%	90%	99%
				Percentiles		
Number of Employees (1970)						
High-Wage Manufacturing	0	17	101	2681	8617	46580
High-Wage Services	2	19	59	602	2601	24044
Low-Wage Manufacturing	0	0	18	605	4509	16003
Low-Wage Services	15	58	113	964	3000	20076
Change in Number of Employees (1978–1970)						
High-Wage Manufacturing	−20926	−1775	−314	87	812	4096
High-Wage Services	−1146	−9	26	920	2982	17358
Low-Wage Manufacturing	−6417	−631	−190	20	153	2296
Low-Wage Services	−2084	−23	22	342	984	4570
Population Size (1970)						
(in 1,000)	1.85	3.74	5.56	31.47	94.74	429.02
Change in Population Size (1980–1970)						
(in 1,000)	−41.56	−1.61	−.04	2.10	5.61	20.06

vided. Table 3.4 includes summaries of the distributions for the population and industry variables. From these distributions, it is evident that outlying observations are present. Hence, means could be biased and standard deviations could be large. The data was checked in order to determine whether the same communities have extreme values across these variables. In general, the same set of communities do not appear as outliers for most of the variables. Due to the absence of a clearly defined subset of cases causing extremeness in scores for most of the variables, deleting cases would not alleviate the problem.

This analysis can make several contributions to the literature since it represents an integration of the different ideas guiding the research presented in the review of the literature in the second chapter. The effects of service sector growth on income are compared with the effects of manufacturing. Also, the impact of change in the different industrial sectors on income levels and its distribution are examined, while controlling for relevant factors such as minorities as a percentage of the population. Past research comparing services and manufacturing has generally failed to simultaneously examine change in these sectors, and in some cases, statistical analyses have not been conducted properly.

The Mid-Atlantic sample used in this study includes a wide range of communities in terms of population size and, to a lesser extent, geographic remoteness. Such variability permits a test of the hypothesis that the growth of services in rural places has a different impact on income than service sector growth occurring in urbanized areas. Most of the studies linking services to income have sampled only metropolitan areas, while studies of rural places generally have focused on economic characteristics of service firms, such as export orientation.

The next chapter describes results from analyses examining the impact of changing employment structures on the level and distribution of income in the Mid-Atlantic communities during the 1970s.

NOTES

1. Two separate analyses are conducted because the appropriate data from the 1990 U.S. census are not yet available for the more detailed community data used in the first analysis.

2. However, the growth rate for the Mid-Atlantic region was lower than the national average.

3. In Pennsylvania, 613 places (49 percent) were classified as rural in the 1980 census. New York had 430 places (45 percent) categorized as rural, while 69 places (15 percent) in New Jersey had a population of 2,500 or less (U.S. Bureau of the Census, 1983: Table 14).

4. Analyses comparing the income distribution for families and unrelated individuals indicate that the distributions for these two groups differ substantially. As a result, income figures for family and unrelated individuals are not merged. In order to limit the scope of an already broad study, I decided to analyze only family income. Families are chosen over unrelated individuals, since families constitute the majority of units in the community by close to a 2:1 ratio in 1980 and a 3:1 ratio in 1970. Refer to Appendix C for a detailed description of results from analyses comparing families and unrelated individuals.

5. The Consumer Price Index with a 1967 base is the basis for making the conversion to constant dollars.

6. Differences exist between the two censuses in some of the ranges used to group income categories for MCDs. These differences are reconciled by converting the endpoints for each category to constant (1982) dollars and then collapsing categories so that comparable income groups are formed for the two years.

The following procedure is used to calculate change in the number of families in the various income groups of the community between 1969 and 1979. First, lower and upper bounds for each income category within each census are converted to 1982 constant dollars. Next, income categories within each census are collapsed in order to form comparable categories between the two censuses.

As a consequence of collapsing income categories, potential differences between groups are hidden and the power of the analysis may be reduced. Changes occurred over the decade in the distribution of income between middle and lower income groups (Browne, 1986), and many of the categories being collapsed are in the lower and middle range of the income distribution. Thus, collapsing income categories results in a conservative bias when deciding if differences exist.

7. Both the lower and middle income groups are comprised of two subgroups. While concern is generally with the "lower class" and "middle class," results from an analysis examining changes in the income distribution indicate that important differences among subgroups in the lower and middle income categories are hidden by collapsing across these subgroups. This analysis is described in Appendix D.

8. New York City and Philadelphia are excluded from these calculations.

9. Manufacturing firms were classified into low-wage and high-wage groups with a procedure similar to that used by Haren (1970). All manufacturing industries, defined by a two-digit 1972 SIC code, within the states of New Jersey, New York, and Pennsylvania were listed in order of average weekly earnings for 1978 and then grouped into homogeneous categories. The Bureau of Labor Statistics was the source of the data. Earnings for 1978 were chosen since the second wave of the Dun and Bradstreet data is for 1978, thereby allowing the most recent estimates to be used in ordering the industries.

10. This list is similar to the one arrived at by Haren (1970). While tobacco, rubber products, and miscellaneous manufacturing industries are not among the lowest-paying industries in his classification scheme, neither are they among the highest-paying industries (Haren, 1970:435–36, Table 2).

11. Nonprofit service industries, such as health and education, tend to have bifurcated earnings and occupational structures (Stanback and Noyelle, 1982:50, Table 3.3). However, these industries are not classified as low-wage services, since wages are not as consistently low as those in the retail and consumer service industries (Stanback and Noyelle, 1982:50).

12. Including all the interaction terms between 1970 employment level and change in employment for each of the four industrial sectors (that is, low- and high-wage manufacturing, low- and high-wage services), induces redundancy in a regression equation. Preliminary analyses indicated that interactions between 1970 employment level and change in employment over the decade for low-wage manufacturing and low-wage services are significantly related to aggregate income, and so these two dependency/change interaction terms were included in the model.

13. The correlation between 1970 population size and the number of families in the lower and upper income segments of the lower income group in 1969 are 0.91 for both. The correlation between the lower and upper segments of the middle income group with population size are 0.95 and 0.99, respectively.

14. The labor market areas were developed by Tolbert and Killian (1987) using commuting data from the 1980 U.S. census.

4

The Impact of Service Sector Employment on Income: The Mid-Atlantic Region from 1969 to 1979

This chapter presents results from analyses of the relationship between increasing employment in the service sector and changes in the level and distribution of income. Communities in the Mid-Atlantic region of the United States provide the sample for the analysis. The analysis of county-level data for the United States as a whole is presented in the fifth chapter.

This chapter is divided into three major sections. The first section describes changes that occurred in the shape of the income distribution in Mid-Atlantic communities during the 1969 to 1979 period. The purpose of the analysis is to examine how the level and distribution of family income changed over the decade.

The second section analyzes the impact of increasing service sector employment on the level and distribution of income in Mid-Atlantic communities. The purpose is to explicitly test whether growth in low-wage and high-wage service sector jobs results in decreased income levels or, alternatively, bipolarization in the income distribution.

The third section examines how the distribution of income is changing between rural and urban communities. Higher-paying administrative and professional jobs tend to centralize in urbanized centers, while jobs requiring less skill, and consequently paying less, locate in rural areas (Porterfield, 1990; Young, 1983). As a result, inequities in the distribution of income across rural and urban communities are expected to increase.

CHANGES IN THE LEVEL AND DISTRIBUTION OF
INCOME: 1969–1979

Some expect a decrease in community income levels to result from a greater reliance on the service sector (for example, see Oregon Joint Legislative Committee, 1984:3). Although median family income increased, on average, across communities in the Mid-Atlantic region during 1969–79,[1] nearly one-half (42 percent) of the communities in the Mid-Atlantic region experienced decline in median family income over the decade. This clearly indicates the presence of a large group of communities that underwent a decline in community income levels while other places experienced gains.

These two trends imply that the distribution of income is changing. Two mechanisms by which income can be redistributed are examined here. First, because some communities experienced decline in median family income while others saw a gain, discrepancies in the availability of resources could be increasing between these two types of places as income is redistributed across communities. Secondly, change in median income *within* a place implies that changes have occurred in that community's own income distribution. The next few paragraphs describe how income was redistributed across communities in the Mid-Atlantic region during the 1969–1979 period.

One way in which income can be redistributed across communities is through changes in the amount of resources flowing to these places, referred to here as a widening of distances. Widening distances between communities imply an increase in inequality in the distribution of income across communities, while narrowing distances imply a reduction in inequality. A second way in which income can be redistributed across communities is through a change in a community's position in the regional hierarchy of places, typically associated with population size. A larger proportion of the resources flow to communities higher in the hierarchy.

By decomposing change in communities' share of income in the region, the extent to which these two sources contribute to the redistribution of income can be determined. The decomposition revealed that there was little change in the distances separating communities.[2] Instead, the major source of change stemmed from communities repositioning or reordering themselves relative to other places in the regional hierarchy. Sixty-four percent of the change that occurred in the distribution of income in the region derives from this source.

In order to measure the actual position of each community in the regional hierarchy, the rank of each community was obtained for 1969 and 1979 in terms of the proportion of family income each contributed to the total for the region. The difference in the community's rank position from 1969 to 1979 (1979–1969) is used to measure change in the position of the community in the hierarchy of places.

As evidenced in Table 4.1, communities in the Mid-Atlantic region jockeyed positions in the income hierarchy. The amount of change communities experi-

Table 4.1
Distributional Characteristics of Change in Position in Regional Income Hierarchy:
1979–1969

Change in Position	Percentile
-101	0% (minimum)
- 61	1%
- 45	5%
- 34	10%
- 17	25%
- 1	50%
13	75%
31	90%
50	95%
74	99%
203	100%

mean: 0   standard deviation: 30
median: -1   inter-quartile range: 30
mode: 3

enced in their rank position varied widely. A value of zero indicates that the community holds the same rank in 1979 as in 1969; only 1.7 percent of the communities experienced no change in their relative positions. Twenty-five percent of the communities experienced minor change in rank by moving no more than five positions up or down the hierarchy. About 68 percent of the communities moved within 30 positions up or down the income hierarchy, as indicated by the standard deviation of 30 and the symmetry of the distribution.

The next few paragraphs describe the redistribution of income *within* Mid-Atlantic communities. Places were classified by the types of changes occurring in the lower, middle, and upper tiers of the community's income distribution. As presented in Table 4.2, the income distribution in 43 percent of the communities moved towards a bifurcated structure, meaning the percentage of families in the lower and upper tiers of the income distribution increased while the percentage in the middle decreased.[3]

In another 33 percent of the communities, the income distribution increased, that is, there was a gain in the number of families in the upper tier while decline occurred in the lower tier. In nearly all of the communities experiencing an increase in the distribution, the percentage of families in the middle income group decreased, meaning the income distribution shifted to the upper end from the middle and lower tiers.[4]

Table 4.2
Classification of Communities by Type of Change in Distribution of Family Income: 1979–1969

Type of Change in Distribution of Income	Percentage
The distribution is ...	
Bifurcating:	
percentage of families decrease in the middle while increasing in lower and upper tiers	42.8%
Increasing:	
percentage of families increase in the upper tier and decrease in the lower tier	33.2
Decreasing:	
percentage of families increase in the lower tier and decrease in the middle and upper tiers	16.2
Other types of changes	7.8
	100.0%

In about 16 percent of the communities in the sample, the distribution of income decreased by moving towards the lower end, that is, the percentage of lower-income families increased, while losses occurred in the middle and upper tiers. About 8 percent of the communities did not f t into any of these change patterns. However, these places appear similar to communities experiencing movement towards the lower end of the distribution. On average, the percentage of families increased in the lower end and middle income tiers and decreased in the upper tier.

Table 4.3 provides a detailed description of communities falling into these categories by listing the average percentage of families in each income group for 1969, 1979, and change over the decade.[5] In order to assess whether the changes occurring in the community income distribution are associated with position in the regional hierarchy or rurality, average change in rank, average community income level, population size, and distance from an interstate highway (a measure of remoteness) are recorded.

Table 4.3
Average Values for Measures of the Level and Distribution of Income and Rurality by Type of Change in Community Income Distribution[a]

Community income distribution is ...

Variable	Bifurcating (n=275) 1969	1979	Change	Increasing (n=213) 1969	1979	Change	Decreasing (n=104) 1969	1979	Change	Other (n=50) 1969	1979	Change	Overall (n=642) 1969	1979	Change
Percentage of Families in Income Groups:[b]															
Lower	14.8	17.3	2.5	20.1	17.2	-2.9	15.4	20.6	5.2	19.6	20.0	0.4	17.0	18.0	1.0
Lowest	10.7	10.8	0.1	14.5	10.5	-4.0	11.1	12.8	1.7	13.7	12.3	-1.4	12.3	11.1	-1.2
Upper-Lower	4.1	6.5	2.4	5.6	6.7	1.1	4.3	7.8	3.5	5.8	7.7	1.9	4.8	6.9	2.1
Middle	65.8	59.7	-6.1	65.2	62.0	-3.2	63.0	59.0	-4.0	61.0	64.0	3.0	64.8	60.7	-4.1
Lower-Middle	35.8	31.5	-4.3	39.2	33.8	-5.4	34.9	33.8	-1.1	34.6	37.9	3.3	36.7	33.1	-3.6
Upper-Middle	30.0	28.1	-1.9	26.0	28.2	2.2	28.0	25.1	-2.9	26.4	26.1	-0.3	28.1	27.5	-0.6
Upper	15.6	18.7	3.1	11.7	17.0	5.3	16.9	15.1	-1.8	15.4	13.0	-2.4	14.5	17.1	2.6
Highest	3.8	4.3	0.5	3.0	3.8	0.8	4.7	5.4	0.7	4.0	2.9	-1.1	3.7	4.2	0.5
Median Family Income	28,988	28,118	1,667	24,994	28,632	6,506	30,815	27,777	-4,658	28,672	27,605	-1,954	28,044	28,129	1,683
Aggregate Income (in $100,000)	1251.6	1532.2	166.2	671.9	903.6	208.3	524.5	610.3	12.5	403.7	397.8	6.5	795.8	973.8	133.2
Rank[c] in Regional Income Hierarchy	398	396	-1	288	302	10	233	224	-15	186	145	-25	--	--	-1
Population Size	17,495	19,839	786	10,435	12,298	831	8,600	9,370	212	5,742	6,108	249	11,632	13,050	576
Distance from Interstate Highway		10			10			10			16			10	

a. Means are presented for most variables. Medians are recorded for those measuring aggregate income, median family income, rank in income hierarchy, population size, and distance of community from interstate highway.

b. Change in percentage points is calculated by subtracting the mean for 1969 from the 1979 value among these variables. For all other variables, change from 1969 to 1979 is calculated from the raw data.

c. The rank of the community with the smallest level of income is one, while the rank with the largest is 642. Also, the median of the ranks for any year is 321.5, discounting ties, for the entire sample.

Communities with an income distribution moving toward the lower end experienced, on average, a decrease in median family income. As would be expected, their relative share of income in the region also tended to decline, indicating a decrease in their rank position in the hierarchy of places. These places tend to have a small population, although they do not appear to differ in terms of remoteness from communities with bifurcating or increasing distributions.

The 50 communities in the "other" category are similar to those characterized as having a decreasing income distribution; they experienced losses in median income and, in addition, underwent considerable decline in rank position within the income hierarchy. These places, on average, tend to have smaller populations and are more remotely located than the other types of communities in the sample.

Conversely, communities with increasing or bifurcating income distributions experienced gains in aggregate and median family income. These communities were able to move up the income hierarchy, or at least remain stable, by claiming a greater share of the income in the region. These trends are most clearly evidenced by communities with an increasing distribution. These communities tended to have moderately sized populations, whereas communities experiencing bifurcation in the income distribution were some of the largest in the region.

Care should be taken not to overstate the strength of the association between population size, remoteness, and the types of changes occurring in the community income distribution. Figures 4.1a and 4.1b depict variation in population size and distance from an interstate highway, respectively, for each type of community. In Figure 4.1a, the lower line represents the population of communities at the 25th percentile (that is, 25 percent of the communities have a population less than or equal to this value). The middle line is the median value (that is, the 50th percentile) as reported in Table 3.3, and the upper line is the population of communities at the 75th percentile. Figure 4.1b can be interpreted similarly in terms of distance from an interstate highway.

Communities undergoing either an increase in the income distribution or classified as "other" are fairly homogeneous in terms of population. The former group tend to be larger places, while the latter are some of the smallest communities in the Mid-Atlantic states. Places classified as "other" can clearly be considered rural since they also tend to be remotely located.

Despite considerable variability in population size among communities with a bifurcating income distribution, these places still tend to have a larger population base than the other types of places. However, communities with a decreasing income distribution include highly populated as well as small communities; these places also vary widely in terms of remoteness of location from an interstate highway.

Summary

These results support the premise that differences are increasing between the smallest places and more urbanized centers. Changes occurred in the rank position

Figure 4.1
Variation in Population Size and Distance to Interstate Highway by Type of Income Distribution

a

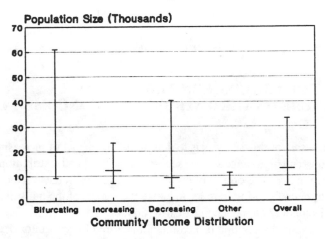

b

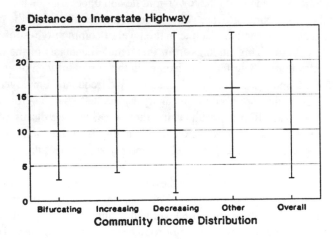

of Mid-Atlantic communities in the income hierarchy despite a lack of change in
the distances separating communities. The smallest places, which tend to be located in more remote areas, appear to have fallen to lower positions in the hierarchy over the decade, in addition to experiencing decreases in the level and distribution of community income. In contrast, larger centers received a greater share
of the income in the region. However, moderately sized places experienced the
biggest gains in income. Among the largest cities, the income distribution either
became more bipolarized or shifted to the lower end.

The next section presents an analysis of the impact of increasing service sector
employment on the level and distribution of community income.

IMPACT OF THE CHANGING INDUSTRIAL STRUCTURE ON THE DISTRIBUTION OF INCOME: 1969-1979

The objective of this analysis is to determine the impact of increasing employment in low- and high-wage service sectors on the level and distribution of income
in the community. The effects of employment changes in these sectors are compared with manufacturing in order to gauge the impact of the transition to a service-based economy on the income distribution.[6]

Change in the distribution of income is measured by growth or decline in the
number of families in different income groups, these being the lower, middle,
upper, and highest strata of the income distribution. The lower income group is
broken down into the lowest and upper-lower income groups, while the middle
income group is divided into the lower-middle and upper-middle income groups,
for a total of six income groups.[7] Change in aggregate income in the community
is used to measure growth or decline in the level of community resources.

To aid in synthesizing findings from this detailed analysis of the community
income distribution, the effects of changes in the community employment structure on income inequality are also estimated. Two frequently employed measures
of income inequality are used in this analysis: the half-share coefficient and the
variance of the logarithms. Results using these measures are discussed briefly in
this section; a detailed discussion of the inequality measures and results is provided in Appendix F, since these findings merely supplement those discussed in
detail here.

Statistical procedures employed in the analyses include robust regression analysis and canonical correlation analysis. The presence of extreme observations, particularly in variables measuring the level and change in employment in services
and manufacturing, warrants the use of robust statistical techniques. The specific
procedure is termed bounded "influence regression"; this term is used inter-
changeably here with "robust regression."[8] A bootstrapping algorithm is used to
estimate the standard errors for the robust regression coefficients.[9] Canonical correlation analysis is used to draw inferences regarding the association between the

combination of changes in service and manufacturing sectors and specific com-
binations of income groups (SAS Institute, Inc., 1985: 139–40).[10]

Results from Regression and Canonical Correlation Analyses

Robust coefficients and asymptotic z-values[11] for the regression models estimating the impact of change in the employment structure on the community income distribution are presented in Table 4.4. Results for six dependent variables
are presented, these being change in the number of families between 1969 and
1979 (1979–1969) in the lowest income group, the upper-lower, the lower-middle, the upper-middle, the upper, and the highest income group. In Table 4.5 the
regression model for predicting change in aggregate community income is presented (See Kassab, 1990c).

All models are statistically significant. Table 4.6 contains the F-value, R^2, and
adjusted R^2 for each model.[12] The large R^2 for each model primarily results from
the association between each dependent variable and population size covariates.[13]

Based on the regression results, Table 4.7 records the change in the number of
families in each income group, given an increase of 100 employees in each industrial sector, controlling for other variables in the model. Similarly, Table 4.8 reports the change expected in aggregate income as a result of one additional employee in a particular industrial sector.

Impact of increasing employment in services.   It is apparent from Table 4.7a
that growth in the high-wage service sector results in a redistribution of families
toward the upper end of the income ladder. Much of the gain occurs in the highest
income group: an increase of 100 employees in this sector is associated with a gain
of 2.4 families in the highest income category. Conversely, an addition of 100
employees in high-wage services leads to declines of approximately two families
in the lowest, upper-lower, and lower middle-income groups. In other words, the
number of families at the extreme upper end of the distribution increases while a
decrease occurs in the number of lower-income families.

This conclusion is supported by results from the canonical correlation analysis
reported in Table 4.9.[14] The first canonical variate indicates that growth in the
high-wage service sector is associated with gains in the highest income group and
declines in the other income categories.[15] These results correspond with the overall effect of change in high-wage services as reported in Table 4.7a.

However, the effect of growth in high-wage services on the upper-middle income group depends on the remoteness of the community, due to the significant
interaction between distance from an interstate highway and growth in the sector,
as shown in the column for the upper-middle income group in Table 4.4. The interaction term indicates that growth in high-wage services results in larger gains
to the upper-middle income group as remoteness of the community increases. For
example, communities 21–35 miles from the interstate highway gain, on average,
5.4 families in the upper-middle income group for each 100 families in high-wage

Table 4.4

Robust Regression Analyses: Predicting Change in the Number of Families in Each Income Group Within the Community

Variables	Lowest Estimate	asymtotic z-value	Upper-Lower Estimate	asymtotic z-value
Intercept	-237.80	-1.3	-60.63	-1.1
Population Size (1970)	-0.00129	-1.3	0.00520	18.4
Quadratic Effect: Population Size (1970)	1.24E-8	6.9	-1.63E-10	-0.3
Change in Population Size (1980 - 1970)	0.00732	1.9	0.00846	7.7
Population Size (1970) x Change in Population	6.93E-8	5.2	3.16E-9	0.9
# Employees in				
High-Wage Manufacturing (1970)	0.00257	0.4	0.00544	3.1
High-Wage Services (1970)	0.02740	3.1	-0.01915	-7.0
Low-Wage Manufacturing (1970)	0.02650	1.9	0.01044	2.2
Low-Wage Services (1970)	-0.02119	-1.1	0.02130	3.9
Change in # Employees:				
High-Wage Manufacturing (1978 - 1970)	-0.01670	-2.1	-0.00570	-2.3
High-Wage Services (1978 - 1970)	-0.02097	-2.8	-0.01646	-6.9
Low-Wage Manufacturing (1978 - 1970)	-0.01199	-0.5	-0.01958	-2.2
Low-Wage Services (1978 - 1970)	0.03871	2.4	0.00044	0.2
# Employees in 1970 x Amount of Change in:				
Low-Wage Manufacturing	---	---	1.90E-6	2.7
Low-Wage Services	-0.00001	-4.8	---	---
Distance from Interstate Highway	0.55799	0.6	-0.35490	-1.3
Distance from Highway x Amount of Change in:				
High-Wage Services (1978 - 1970)	---	---	---	---
Low-Wage Services (1978 - 1970)	-0.00246	-1.7	---	---
Service-based Economy Dummy	3.97310	0.1	-0.07611	-0.0
Percentage of Employees in				
HQ Firms in LMA (1970)	-4.20084	-1.8	-2.33723	-3.1
Median Value of Home	0.00081	0.7	-0.00197	-6.0
Percentage in 1970:				
Females in Work Force	7.15325	1.6	3.21219	2.3
Minority Population	10.79268	3.1	0.91802	0.8
Elderly Population	-6.90800	-1.3	3.04875	1.8
Percentage Change between 1970 and 1980:				
Females in Work Force	0.93220	1.3	0.32874	1.6
Minority Population	0.03076	0.7	-0.01589	-1.2
Elderly Population	0.32124	0.4	0.95111	4.5
Percentage (Number) of Cases Downweighted:	7.3 (47)		7.9 (51)	

Table 4.4 continued

Variables	Lower-Middle Estimate	Lower-Middle asymtotic z-value	Upper-Middle Estimate	Upper-Middle asymtotic z-value
Intercept	-1150.91	-4.3	670.82	3.1
Population Size (1970)	-0.00477	-3.3	0.00105	0.9
Quadratic Effect: Population Size (1970)	2.44E-8	10.4	-1.92E-8	-8.4
Change in Population Size (1980 - 1970)	0.04463	8.0	0.09005	18.0
Population Size (1970) x Change in Population	1.32E-7	7.6	-1.54E-7	-8.9
# Employees in				
High-Wage Manufacturing (1970)	-0.02557	-2.9	-0.00585	-0.8
High-Wage Services (1970)	-0.03576	-3.0	-0.04970	-4.6
Low-Wage Manufacturing (1970)	-0.02929	-1.4	-0.01358	-0.8
Low-Wage Services (1970)	0.04036	1.4	0.01090	0.4
Change in # Employees:				
High-Wage Manufacturing (1978 - 1970)	0.00203	0.2	0.01176	1.1
High-Wage Services (1978 - 1970)	-0.01915	-1.8	-0.03549	-3.6
Low-Wage Manufacturing (1978 - 1970)	0.05485	1.5	-0.02175	-0.7
Low-Wage Services (1978 - 1970)	0.04952	3.1	-0.05763	-3.0
# Employees in 1970 x Amount of Change in:				
Low-Wage Manufacturing	---	---	---	---
Low-Wage Services	---	---	0.00001	5.8
Distance from Interstate Highway	0.29000	0.2	-1.95195	-1.6
Distance from Highway x Amount of Change in:				
High-Wage Services (1978 - 1970)	---	---	0.00319	3.6
Low-Wage Services (1978 - 1970)	---	---	0.00391	2.3
Service-based Economy Dummy	14.29417	0.3	6.29577	0.2
Percentage of Employees in				
HQ Firms in LMA (1970)	-0.08840	-0.0	2.88977	1.0
Median Value of Home	0.00614	3.4	-0.00564	-4.1
Percentage in 1970:				
Females in Work Force	21.39870	3.1	-11.39605	-2.0
Minority Population	-10.41496	-2.0	-3.75193	-0.8
Elderly Population	10.74661	1.3	1.33566	0.2
Percentage Change between 1970 and 1980:				
Females in Work Force	1.06876	1.0	-1.29980	-1.4
Minority Population	-0.02290	-0.3	-0.06827	-1.2
Elderly Population	1.99357	1.7	0.71932	0.7
Percentage (Number) of Cases Downweighted:	7.3 (47)		8.6 (55)	

Table 4.4 continued

Variables	Estimate	Upper asymtotic z-value	Estimate	Highest asymtotic z-value
Intercept	839.19	3.5	174.61	1.5
Population Size (1970)	0.01257	10.0	0.00517	8.0
Quadratic Effect: Population Size (1970)	-1.60E-8	-6.8	-6.77E-9	-6.5
Change in Population Size (1980 - 1970)	0.09706	18.3	0.02099	8.4
Population Size (1970) x Change in				
Population	-1.42E-7	-7.7	-3.42E-8	-4.3
# Employees in				
High-Wage Manufacturing (1970)	0.04142	5.4	0.00909	2.3
High-Wage Services (1970)	-0.07359	-5.6	-0.02600	-4.3
Low-Wage Manufacturing (1970)	-0.03749	-1.8	-0.01813	-1.8
Low-Wage Services (1970)	-0.06877	-2.9	-0.05286	-4.2
Change in # Employees:				
High-Wage Manufacturing (1978 - 1970)	0.03879	3.4	0.00949	1.7
High-Wage Services (1978 - 1970)	-0.01102	-1.1	0.02392	4.5
Low-Wage Manufacturing (1978 - 1970)	0.00803	0.2	0.05429	2.7
Low-Wage Services (1978 - 1970)	-0.03487	-1.8	-0.01466	-2.1
# Employees in 1970 x Amount of Change in:				
Low-Wage Manufacturing	-0.00001	-2.1	-0.00001	-4.1
Low-Wage Services	5.81E-6	2.4	---	---
Distance from Interstate Highway	0.09425	0.1	0.82227	1.3
Distance from Highway x Amount of Change in:				
High-Wage Services (1978 - 1970)	---	---	---	---
Low-Wage Services (1978 - 1970)	---	---	---	---
Service-based Economy Dummy	0.52522	0.0	-3.13329	-0.2
Percentage of Employees in				
HQ Firms in LMA (1970)	3.25317	1.0	3.33056	2.1
Median Value of Home	-0.00354	-2.3	0.00283	3.8
Percentage in 1970:				
Females in Work Force	-16.69493	-2.6	-8.12721	-2.6
Minority Population	-0.51113	-0.1	-2.51995	-1.0
Elderly Population	-13.17182	-1.8	-3.07179	-0.8
Percentage Change between 1970 and 1980:				
Females in Work Force	-1.06537	-1.1	-0.82148	-1.6
Minority Population	-0.01448	-0.2	0.01267	0.4
Elderly Population	-0.35847	-0.4	-0.21101	-0.4

Percentage (Number) of Cases Downweighted: 7.9 (51)   8.7 (56)

Table 4.5
Robust Regression Analyses: Predicting Change in Community Aggregate Income

Variables	Estimate	asymptotic z-value
Intercept	57203404.36	2.7
Population Size (1970)	1152.1025	9.6
Quadratic Effect: Population Size (1970)	-0.00153000	-7.0
Change in Population Size (1980 - 1970)	9914.5732	20.2
Population Size (1970) x Change in Population	-0.00803829	-4.9
# Employees in		
High-Wage Manufacturing (1970)	1536.8581	2.2
High-Wage Services (1970)	-6290.3551	-5.6
Low-Wage Manufacturing (1970)	-3212.0961	-1.6
Low-Wage Services (1970)	-10538.8466	-4.9
Change in # Employees:		
High-Wage Manufacturing (1978 - 1970)	2510.7921	2.5
High-Wage Services (1978 - 1970)	1752.1486	1.8
Low-Wage Manufacturing (1978 - 1970)	5498.6765	1.5
Low-Wage Services (1978 - 1970)	-5314.5723	-2.6
# Employees in 1970 x Amount of Change in:		
Low-Wage Manufacturing	-0.98249368	-3.7
Low-Wage Services	0.79516654	3.7
Distance from Interstate Highway	-2848.6851	-0.0
Distance from Highway x Amount of Change in:		
High-Wage Services (1978 - 1970)	205.7887	2.3
Low-Wage Services (1978 - 1970)	306.2082	1.7
Service-based Economy Dummy	-1342160.95	-0.4
Percentage of Employees in		
HQ Firms in LMA (1970)	598767.94	2.1
Median Value of Home	-16.6806	-0.1
Percentage in 1970:		
Females in Work Force	-1482888.59	-2.7
Minority Population	-665570.06	-1.5
Elderly Population	-844688.68	-1.3
Percentage Change between 1970 and 1980:		
Females in Work Force	-93423.77	-1.1
Minority Population	-1404.73	-0.3
Elderly Population	41347.07	0.5

Percentage (Number) of Cases Downweighted: 8.9 (57)
Source: Kassab, 1990c

Table 4.6
Statistics Assessing Significance of Models

Model	F-value	degrees of freedom	R^2	adjusted R^2
Change in Number of Families in Each Income Category:				
Lowest Income Group	38.017[*]	24, 617	0.60	0.58
Upper-Lower	372.501[*]	23, 618	0.93	0.93
Lower-Middle	146.569[*]	22, 619	0.84	0.83
Upper-Middle	220.877[*]	25, 616	0.90	0.90
Upper	57.822[*]	24, 617	0.69	0.68
Highest	38.365[*]	23, 618	0.59	0.57
Change in Aggregate Income	168.15[*]	26, 615	0.88	0.87

[*] $p < 0.0001$

services. On the other hand, a gain of 100 families in high-wage services among centrally located places is associated with a loss of 3.5 families in this income category. This relationship is charted in Table 4.7b.

Consistent with these findings, employment growth in the high-wage service sector leads to gains in community aggregate income. However, the effect is strongest for remotely located communities, due to the significant interaction term between high-wage services and distance from an interstate highway (refer to Table 4.5). For instance, among communities located more than 35 miles from an interstate highway, an additional job in high-wage services is worth over $12,000 to the community in terms of aggregate income. Conversely, employment growth in high-wage services has a negligible impact in aggregate income in centrally located places (see Table 4.8b).

Hence, among more rural communities, growth in high-wage services has a beneficial impact on both income and its distribution. But among centrally located places, high-wage service sector growth does not appear to have much effect on aggregate income levels. However, growth in this sector is associated with increasing inequality, since only those in the highest income group benefit from employment gains.

Table 4.7
Change in Number of Families in Each Income Group with an Increase of 100 Employees in an Industry

Panel a: Average Effect of Increasing the Number of Employees by 100

Industry Variables[a]	Change in Number of Families in Each Income Group					
	Lowest	Upper Lower	Lower Middle	Upper Middle	Upper	Highest
Change in Manufacturing (1978 - 1970)						
High-Wage	-1.7	-0.6 [b]	0.2(ns)	1.2 [b]	3.9 [b]	0.9(ns) [b]
Low-Wage	-1.2(ns)		5.5(ns)	-2.2(ns)		
Change in Services (1978 - 1970)						
High-Wage	-2.1 [b]	-1.6	-1.9	-0.4 [b]	-1.1(ns) [b]	2.4
Low-Wage		0(ns)	5.0			-1.5

ns not significant at the .05 level

Panel b: Change in Number of Families in Each Income Group with an Increase of 100 Employees in High-Wage Services, Grouped by Distance from Interstate Highway

Distance from Highway	Lowest	Upper Lower	Lower Middle	Upper Middle	Upper	Highest
0 Miles:						
Change in High-Wage Serv.	-2.1	-1.6	-1.9	-3.5	-1.1(ns)	2.4
1-3 Miles:						
Change in High-Wage Serv.	"	"	"	-2.9	"	"
4-10 Miles:						
Change in High-Wage Serv.	"	"	"	-1.3	"	"
11-20 Miles:						
Change in High-Wage Serv.	"	"	"	1.2	"	"
21-35 Miles:						
Change in High-Wage Serv.	"	"	"	5.4	"	"
Over 35 Miles:						
Change in High-Wage Serv.	"	"	"	13.0	"	"

a. Explanatory variables were evaluated at the median.
b. Variable is part of interaction term for this dependent variable.

Table 4.7 continued

Panel c: Change in Number of Families in Each Income Group with an Increase of 100 Employees in Low-Wage Services, Grouped by Distance from Interstate Highway

Distance from Highway	Lowest	Upper Lower	Lower Middle	Upper Middle	Upper	Highest
0 Miles:						
Change in Low-Wage Serv.	3.6	0(ns)	5.0	-5.4	-3.3	-1.5
1-3 Miles:						
Change in Low-Wage Serv.	3.1	"	"	-4.6	"	"
4-10 Miles:						
Change in Low-Wage Serv.	1.9	"	"	-2.6	"	"
11-20 Miles:						
Change in Low-Wage Serv.	0.1	"	"	0.5	"	"
21-35 Miles:						
Change in Low-Wage Serv.	-3.3	"	"	5.6	"	"
Over 35 Miles:						
Change in Low-Wage Serv.	-9.2	"	"	15.0	"	"

Panel d: Change in Number of Families in Each Income Group with an Increase of 100 Employees in Low-Wage Services, Grouped by Number of Employees in Low-wage Services in 1970 (n=642)

1970 Level: Low-Wage Serv.	Lowest	Upper Lower	Lower Middle	Upper Middle	Upper	Highest
Low (100)[a]:						
Change in Low-Wage Serv.	1.3	0(ns)	5.0	-1.7	-3.4	-1.5
Medium (350):						
Change in Low-Wage Serv.	1.1	"	"	-1.4	-3.3	"
High (1,000):						
Change in Low-Wage Serv.	0.6	"	"	-0.5	-2.9	"
Very High (3,000):						
Change in Low-Wage Serv.	-1.1	"	"	2.1	-1.7	"

a. The categories, low, medium, high, and very high represent approximately the 20th, 50th, 75th, and 90th percentiles, respectively; numbers in parentheses are the number of employees at these levels. Similar procedures were followed in panel (e).

Table 4.7 continued

Panel e: Change in Number of Families in Each Income Group with an Increase
of 100 Employees in Low-Wage Manufacturing, Grouped by Number of Employees
in Low-wage Services in 1970 (n=642)

1970 Level: Low-Wage Serv.	Lowest	Upper Lower	Lower Middle	Upper Middle	Upper	Highest
Low (10):						
Change in Low-Wage Manu.	-1.2(ns)	-2.0	5.5(ns)	-2.2(ns)	0.8	5.4
Medium (150):						
Change in Low-Wage Manu.	"	-1.9	"	"	0.7	5.3
High (600):						
Change in Low-Wage Manu.	"	-1.8	"	"	0.4	5.0
Very High (2,100):						
Change in Low-Wage Manu.	"	-1.6	"	"	-0.6	4.0

The effect of low-wage service sector growth on the income distribution depends on the centrality or remoteness of the community's location, as indicated by the statistical significance of the interaction terms listed in Table 4.4. For centrally located places, growth in the low-wage service sector is associated with increased numbers in the lowest segment of the income distribution and decreased numbers in the upper-middle income group (refer to Table 4.7c). Growth in this sector among centrally located places also results in declines in aggregate income; this effect is evidenced from the significant interaction between growth in low-wage services and distance from an interstate highway (see Tables 4.5 and 4.8c). Thus growth in this low-paying sector in centrally located places results in a loss of income as families are redistributed towards the lower end of the income ladder.

However, this negative effect weakens as remoteness increases. In fact, for about 35 percent of the Mid-Atlantic communities located more than 15 miles from an interstate highway, growth in low-wage services results in a decrease in the number of families in the lowest income group. In addition, the number of families in the upper-middle income group tends to increase. This means that income is being redistributed toward the middle income brackets. However, only the most remotely located communities experience gains in aggregate income (See Table 4.8c).

The significant interaction between the initial level of low-wage services and subsequent growth in this sector indicates that the negative impact of growth in the sector declines as its initial size becomes bigger. When initial employment in low-wage services is low, growth in this sector is more strongly associated with

Table 4.8
Change in Community Aggregate Income with an Increase of One Employee in an Industry

Panel a: Industry Variables[a]	Overall Average Effect
Change in Manufacturing (1978-1970)	
High-Wage	2511
Low-Wage	5350
Change in Services (1978-1970)	
High-Wage	3810
Low-Wage	-2001

Panel b: Change in Community Aggregate Income with an Increase of One Employee in High-Wage Services, Grouped by Distance from Interstate Highway (n=642)

Distance from Highway	Robust Effect
0 Miles:	
Change in High-Wage Services (1978-1970)	1752
1-3 Miles:	
Change in High-Wage Services (1978-1970)	2164
4-10 Miles:	
Change in High-Wage Services (1978-1970)	3193
11-20 Miles:	
Change in High-Wage Services (1978-1970)	4839
21-35 Miles:	
Change in High-Wage Services (1978-1970)	7514
Over 35 Miles:	
Change in High-Wage Services (1978-1970)	12453

Panel c: Change in Community Aggregate Income with an Increase of One Employee in Low-Wage Services, Grouped by Distance from Interstate Highway (n=642)

Distance from Highway	Robust Effect
0 Miles:	
Change in Low-Wage Services (1978-1970)	-5063
1-3 Miles:	
Change in Low-Wage Services (1978-1970)	-4451
4-10 Miles:	
Change in Low-Wage Services (1978-1970)	-2920
11-20 Miles:	
Change in Low-Wage Services (1978-1970)	-470
21-35 Miles:	
Change in Low-Wage Services (1978-1970)	3511
Over 35 Miles:	
Change in Low-Wage Services (1978-1970)	10860

Table 4.8 continued

Panel d: Change in Community Aggregate Income with an Increase of One Employee in Low-Wage Services, Grouped by Number of Employees in Low-Wage Services in 1970 (n=642)

1970 Level of Low-Wage Services[b]	Robust Effect
Low:	
Change in Low-Wage Services (1978-1970)	-2173
Medium:	
Change in Low-Wage Services (1978-1970)	-1974
High:	
Change in Low-Wage Services (1978-1970)	-1457

Panel e: Change in Community Aggregate Income with an Increase of One Employee in Low-Wage Manufacturing, Grouped by Number of Employees in Low-Wage Manufacturing in 1970 (n=642)

1970 Level of Low-Wage Manufacturing	Robust Effect
Low:	
Change in Low-Wage Manu. (1978-1970)	5489
Medium:	
Change in Low-Wage Manu. (1978-1970)	5351
High:	
Change in Low-Wage Manu. (1978-1970)	4909

a. Explanatory variables are evaluated at the median.

b. The categories low, medium, and high, represent approximately the 20th, 50th, and 75th percentiles, respectively.

Source: Kassab, 1990c

Table 4.9
**Canonical Correlation Analysis: Change in the Number of Families in Each Income
Group with Change in Each Industrial Sector**

Panel a: Standardized Canonical Coefficients

Variables	First Variate	Second Variate	Third Variate
Change in # Families (1979-1969):			
Lowest Income Group	-0.5568	0.5526	-0.0177
Upper-Lower Income Group	-0.4974	0.1985	-0.0962
Lower-Middle Income Group	-0.2847	-0.0456	1.0973
Upper-Middle Income Group	-0.5824	-0.0890	0.4455
Upper Income Group	-0.5675	-0.5345	0.0378
Highest Income Group	0.4514	0.2266	0.1558
Change in # Employees (1978-1970):			
High-Wage Manufacturing	0.1033	-0.9864	0.0136
High-Wage Services	0.9721	0.2271	-0.2297
Low-Wage Manufacturing	0.1547	0.2220	0.6548
Low-Wage Services	-0.1675	-0.3969	0.7100

Panel b: Raw Canonical Coefficients

Variables	First Variate	Second Variate	Third Variate
Change in # Families (1979-1969):			
Lowest Income Group	-0.0025	0.0025	-0.0001
Upper-Lower Income Group	-0.0056	0.0022	-0.0011
Lower-Middle Income Group	-0.0008	-0.0001	0.0030
Upper-Middle Income Group	-0.0019	-0.0003	0.0015
Upper Income Group	-0.0018	-0.0017	0.0001
Highest Income Group	0.0027	0.0014	0.0009
Change in # Employees (1978-1970):			
High-Wage Manufacturing	0.0001	-0.0006	9.1E-6
High-Wage Services	0.0008	0.0002	-0.0002
Low-Wage Manufacturing	0.0003	0.0005	0.0015
Low-Wage Services	-0.0002	-0.0005	0.0009

increased numbers in the lowest income groups and a loss of families in the upper-middle and upper income groups. Conversely, declines in aggregate income are less likely to occur when the initial level of employment in this sector is considerable (refer to Tables 4.7d and 4.8d).[16]

Over 60 percent of the communities with more than 3,000 employees in low-wage services have a diversified local economy; in contrast, only 34 percent of the communities in the entire sample are diversified. Continued growth in low-wage services most likely reflects the positive effect of a diversified economy. Growth in other sectors of the local economy such as manufacturing, construction, or government acts to increase income levels and promote growth in low-wage services.

In summary, findings from the robust regressions and canonical correlation analyses indicate that the impact of the service sector on the level and distribution of income in the community depends upon the remoteness of the community. Among more remote places, growth in services as a whole results in increased aggregate income and an expansion of the middle income group. Low-wage services, in particular, are associated with a decreased number of families in the lowest income group but increased numbers in the lower-middle and upper-middle income groups.[17] For centrally located places, on the other hand, growth in the service sector is associated with declines in aggregate income and increasing bipolarization of the income distribution, as numbers in the lower and highest segments of the distribution increase.

Gains (or declines) in community aggregate income tend to respond to corresponding changes in the number of families in the middle income groups. This means that structural changes that affect the middle of the income distribution are more likely to affect the level of aggregate income in the community. This is probably due to the large proportion of families in the middle of the income distribution (see Table 4.3).

Impact of changing employment in manufacturing. Results reported in Tables 4.4, 4.5, 4.7a, and 4.8a indicate that employment losses in high-wage manufacturing adversely affect aggregate income levels and the number of families in the upper-middle and upper income groups. A loss of one job in high-wage manufacturing is associated with a decrease of $2,500 in aggregate income for the community (refer to Table 4.8a). The decline associated with a loss in employment in this sector on community income is probably limited because other sources of income are substituted for lost manufacturing wages, such as union unemployment benefits.

A loss of 100 jobs in high-wage manufacturing is expected to result in four families leaving the upper income group and 1.2 families leaving the upper-middle. Conversely, the number of families in the lowest income group increases by 1.2 for every 100 jobs lost in this sector. Declines in high-wage manufacturing also result in a redistribution of families towards the lower end of the income ladder.

Results from the canonical correlation analysis reported in Table 4.9 support the inference that employment losses in high-wage manufacturing are associated with a decline in the number of families in the upper income group and an increase in the number in the lowest income group. In addition, results from the regression model used to predict change in the level of inequality over the decade, reported in Appendix F, indicate that dependency on this sector leads to increased income inequality, as defined by the variance of the logarithms. This effect is consistent with results indicating a loss of families in the upper income groups, and would be due to declining employment in the sector.

Referring again to Table 4.7a, regression results indicate that gains in low-wage manufacturing affect both the upper and lower half of the community income distribution. A gain of 100 employees in this sector results in an additional 5.3 families in the highest income group, although the effect on the upper income group is minor. Aggregate income also tends to increase as a result of employment gains in low-wage manufacturing (refer to Table 4.8a).

Growth in low-wage manufacturing also leads to a significant reduction in the number of families in the upper end of the lower income group. An increase of 100 employees in the sector is expected to result in a loss of nearly two families in the upper-lower income group.

While the effects for low-wage manufacturing are not statistically significant for either the lower-middle or upper-middle income groups, the magnitudes of the effects are large. For instance, the robust regression estimate for the lower-middle income group means that an increase of 100 employees in low-wage manufacturing would result in an additional 5.5 families in that income group. The lack of statistical significance indicates considerable inconsistency in the effect of this sector on change in the middle income groups, since the standard errors for the variables are large relative to the estimated size of the effect across communities.

Results from the canonical correlation analysis reported in Table 4.9 hint at the reason for the inconsistent effect. Coefficients from the third variate indicate that the combination of increasing employment in these two low-wage sectors is associated with substantial gains in the middle income group, particularly the lower-middle. This means that the combination of employment growth in low-wage services and manufacturing leads to families being redistributed toward the lower middle portion of the income distribution and, to a lesser extent, the upper-middle income group.[18]

In addition, the impact of employment growth in low-wage manufacturing on the level of income and its distribution depends upon the initial prevalence of that sector in the local economy, due to the significant interactions reported in Tables 4.4 and 4.5. For communities with a smaller number of employees in low-wage manufacturing, an increase of 100 employees is associated with bigger gains in the upper portion of the distribution and larger declines in the upper-lower income group. Similarly, the significant interaction between prevalence of this sector and subsequent growth indicates that the positive effect of growth in low-wage manufacturing on aggregate income increases as prevalence of the sector declines (refer to Table 4.8e). Recall that the corresponding effect for low-wage services moves in the opposite direction—the greater the prevalence of low-wage services in the local economy, the more positive the effect subsequent growth has on income.

One reason for these results could be that places with a smaller number employed in low-wage manufacturing also tend to be smaller in population size ($r =$ 0.62, $p < .0001$).[19] Smaller communities are more likely to benefit from growth in this sector since the opportunity for employment in other industries, such as services or government, is less in these places. Thus, a job in low-wage manufacturing may be worth more in a rural community than in a more populated area.

Comparison of Services and Manufacturing as Sources of Employment: Implications for Economic Development

Figure 4.2 provides a visual comparison of the estimated effect of each industrial sector on different income groups. But, the effect of service sector growth varies by remoteness of location for the lowest and upper-middle income groups. These results are pictured in Figures 4.3 and 4.4, respectively. In Figure 4.5, the estimated effect on aggregate income is illustrated for communities varying by remoteness of location.[20]

Low-wage manufacturing and low-wage services appear to have a similar effect on the lower and middle income groups among more remote places (see Figure 4.2). Growth in low-wage services leads to reductions in the number of families in the lowest income group and gains in aggregate income for remotely located communities (see Figures 4.3 and 4.5). Furthermore, low-wage services have a strong positive impact on both the lower middle and upper middle-income groups among these places (see Figures 4.2 and 4.4). This sector appears to do a better job of improving economic well-being among these places than low- or high-wage manufacturing or high-wage services.

However, among centrally located places, growth in low-wage services is associated with a decrease in aggregate income as the income distribution shifts to the lower end (refer to Figure 4.5). Specifically, declines occur in the number of families at the upper end, while the lower end increases in number (See Figures 4.3 and 4.4).

Among centrally located places, high-wage services and high-wage manufacturing appear to be fairly similar in their effect on aggregate income as well as the lower and upper ends of the income distribution. But among remotely located communities, the positive impact of both low-wage and high-wage services on aggregate income and the upper middle-income group exceeds the impact of employment growth in high-wage manufacturing (see Figures 4.3, 4.4, and 4.5).

The analyses highlight the potential of both low- and high-wage service sectors as a resource tool among more remotely located communities. However, many of these places are dependent upon low-wage branch manufacturing with minimal development of the service sector.[21] Whether employment growth in the high-wage service sector acts to reduce or widen the gap in resources between urban and rural places is uncertain. This sector has a more beneficial impact on income in remote communities, but growth in the sector is more likely in urbanized areas ($r = 0.72$).

Because growth in low-wage services has been fairly ubiquitous across communities with different population sizes, it may prove to be the most accessible means for narrowing, or at least maintaining, the gap in resources between rural and urban communities.[22] Thus, low-wage services may constitute the most probable means of inducing economic development and resource growth in smaller and more remotely located places.

The positive impact of service sector growth on the local economy of remote communities indicates that this sector has the potential to induce economic devel-

Figure 4.2
Change in Income Groups by Industry

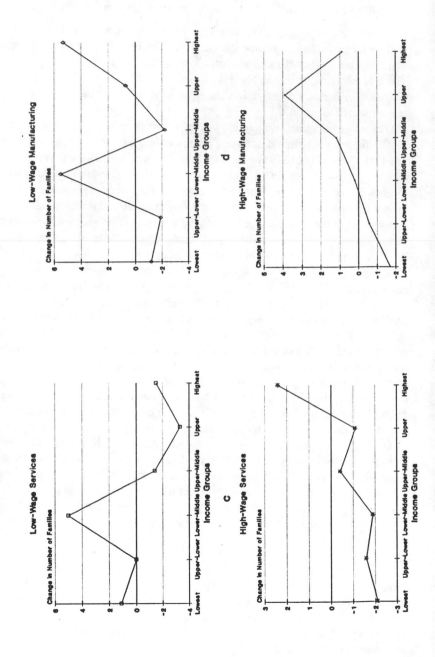

74

Figure 4.3
Change in Lowest Income Group by Industry and Distance from an Interstate Highway

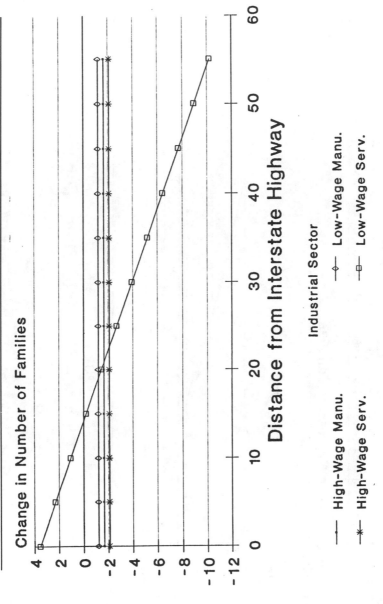

Figure 4.4
Change in Upper-Middle Income Group by Industry and Distance from an Interstate Highway

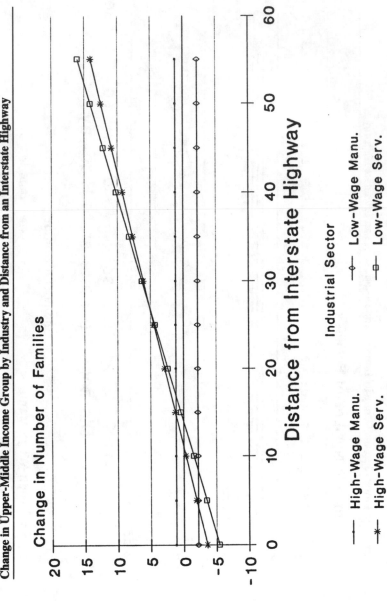

Change in Number of Families

Distance from Interstate Highway

Industrial Sector

— High-Wage Manu.   —◇— Low-Wage Manu.

—*— High-Wage Serv.   —□— Low-Wage Serv.

Figure 4.5
Change in Aggregate Income by Industry and Remoteness

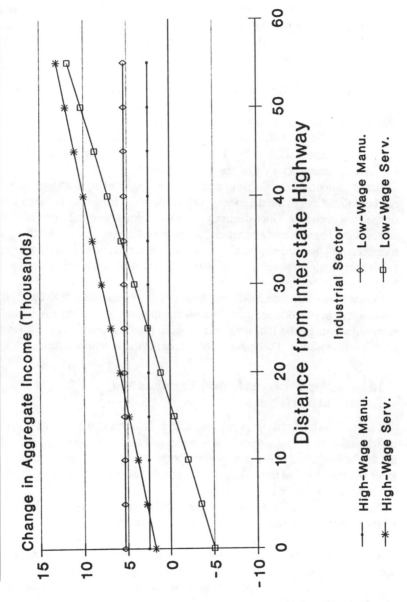

Change in Aggregate Income (Thousands)

Distance from Interstate Highway

Industrial Sector

— High–Wage Manu.   — Low–Wage Manu.

—*— High–Wage Serv.   —□— Low–Wage Serv.

opment and a more equitable distribution of income within the community. However, more remote communities have tended to experience greater gains, or at least fewer losses, in low-wage and high-wage manufacturing over the decade ($r = 0.11, p < .01$ for both relationships). At least under these conditions, the service sector is able to promote the economic well-being of the community. The extent to which these effects are dependent on growth (or decline) in manufacturing is uncertain.

Centrally located communities, on the other hand, have tended to experience growth in both low-wage and high-wage service sectors while undergoing considerable decline in low-wage and high-wage manufacturing sectors (refer to Table H.1 in Appendix H). One reason for the negative impact of the service sector on the level and distribution of income could be the depressing effect of large-scale job losses in manufacturing on the local economy.[23]

Hence, potential benefits from gains in low-wage and high-wage services may not be realized due to the dampening effects of major job losses in manufacturing on the local economy. Once declines in manufacturing have stabilized, the service sector should have a more beneficial influence on the income distribution among more centrally located places. Promoting continued growth in the service sector, particularly high-wage services, may provide a feasible approach to economic development for these places.

Communities located a moderate distance from an interstate highway appear to have experienced moderate gains in low- and high-wage services and small losses in manufacturing. The industrial mix in these places appears to have a favorable impact on the level and distribution of income in these communities.

Relationship between Control Variables and Dependent Variables

The relationship between population size and change in the income distribution indicates that larger population size is associated with increasing numbers of families at the lower and upper ends of the income distribution (see Table 4.4). Also, more centrally located places experienced increases in income inequality (refer to Table F.1 in Appendix F).

Past a certain size, however, a larger population is associated with decreasing numbers in the upper portion of the distribution. Hence, it appears that in the largest places, families are being redistributed toward the lower income brackets, while moderate-sized cities are experiencing increasing bifurcation (see Table 4.4). Consistent with these findings, the largest places experienced declines in aggregate income over the decade, as indicated by the significant quadratic term for population size in Table 4.5.

The significant interaction term between 1970 population size and change in population over the decade when the dependent variable is aggregate income indicates that additional population growth provides a higher dollar return for smaller communities than larger ones. Consistent with this result, the corresponding interaction terms in Table 4.4 imply that larger places in 1970 found population growth to be associated with increased numbers of families in the lower half of the income distribution, while the number of families in the upper half declined. These results suggest that continued population growth has a diminishing return for the community.

Communities with higher percentages of females in the work force also experienced a redistribution of families toward the lower end of the scale, as the number of families in the upper-lower and lower-middle income groups increased and the number in the upper income group decreased. Consistent with the tendency for homogeneity of income to increase, income inequality tends to decrease in places with higher proportions of women in the work force (Table F.1 in Appendix F). Also, a larger percentage of women in the work force is negatively associated with gains in aggregate income (see Table 4.5), thereby reflecting the tendency for women to occupy lower-paying positions (Browne, 1986:22–23).

Similarly, a higher proportion of elderly in the population is associated with gains in the upper-lower and lower-middle section of the income distribution. These findings are consistent with the idea that much of the elderly population, while above the poverty line, may be experiencing financial hardship. Income inequality also tended to increase when a larger proportion of the population was elderly (see Table F.1 in Appendix F).

A higher percentage of minorities in the population is associated with increasing levels of inequality, as is a larger gain in the minority population, based on the analysis of the variance of the logarithms reported in Table F.1 in Appendix F. Increased financial hardship in these communities is evidenced by the increased number of families in the lowest income group and the decreased number of families in the lower-middle income group (refer to Table 4.4).

The percentage of workers employed in headquarters firms in the community's labor market area (LMA) has a positive effect on aggregate income levels, indicating that the flow of dollars to areas possessing greater corporate control over the activity of firms is greater (see Table 4.5). Communities in regions with more headquarters activity are in a better position to direct resources back to the community. In addition, communities in LMAs with higher percentages of workers employed in headquarters firms tend to have lower levels of inequality (see Table F.1).

Places in which the median value of homes in the community is higher (that is, those places with higher standards of living), saw a decrease in the level of income inequality (see Table F.1). This may be a result, however, of the higher cost of living pushing families in the lower income groups out of the community.

The next section reports results from an analysis of change in the distribution of aggregate income across communities in the Mid-Atlantic states.

IMPACT OF THE CHANGING INDUSTRIAL STRUCTURE ON POSITION IN THE REGIONAL HIERARCHY: 1969–1979

The objective of this section is to determine whether discrepancies between communities in the regional hierarchy in the distribution of income are increasing or decreasing as local economies become more service-based. Change in the rank of the community in the regional hierarchy is the dependent variable.

Table 4.10 lists results from the regression model used to examine the impact of change in the industrial structure on change in the community's rank in the income hierarchy. In contrast to the models presented in the prior section, this model contains a variable measuring the interaction between population size and percentage change in female labor force participation.[24] Also, the ordinary least squares (OLS) results are reported for this model, rather than the bounded influence (that is, robust) results, since differences between the OLS and robust regressions were minimal.

Several points are highlighted by the analysis. First, none of the variables measuring number of employees or change in employees in low-wage or high-wage services are significant. This means that increasing reliance on the service sector does not impact *directly* on the redistribution of income across communities in the region.

However, results do indicate that a decrease in employment in high-wage manufacturing leads to a loss of position in the regional income hierarchy, although this effect is weak ($p < .08$). In addition, the coefficient for the dummy variable measuring whether a place is dependent on high-wage branch manufacturing indicates that these places decreased in rank by approximately four positions over the decade, ($p < .08$). Thus, it appears that communities dependent on high-wage branch manufacturing, a sector experiencing large job losses during the 1969–1979 period, tended to decrease in position in the income hierarchy.

These results highlight the negative impact of job losses in manufacturing on the community's economic stability, particularly for those communities highly dependent on that sector. Promoting manufacturing development in a local economy to the extent that the community becomes highly dependent on the sector for employment places the community in a precarious position if that sector undergoes decline.[25] Recall from the prior section that these places also experienced an increase in income inequality.

The effect of population size on change in the community's rank in the income hierarchy indicates that disparities in the distribution of income are increasing between smaller communities and larger ones. Smaller places have tended to decline in rank, while medium-sized places moved up the hierarchy. In addition, the largest places declined in rank, as indicated by the significant quadratic effect.[26] Hence, the hierarchy of places, in terms of the distribution of resources associated with population size, appears to have solidified for the majority of places.

This effect may be due, at least partially, to the differential location of producer and consumer services over different-sized places. Higher-paying producer services have tended to locate in larger places, while lower-paying consumer services have been more evenly distributed across space (Gillespie and Green, 1987; Hirschl and McReynolds, 1989; Miller and Bluestone, 1987).[27] These findings imply that growth in the service economy *indirectly* leads to increasing levels of

Table 4.10
OLS Regression Analysis: Predicting Change in Community's Rank in the Income Hierarchy: 1979–1969

Variables	Estimate	t-value
Intercept	-1.6166	-0.2
Rank in 1969	-0.0428	-6.0
Population Size (1970)	0.0004	5.1
Quadratic Effect: Population Size (1970)	-1.92E-10	-3.2
Change in Population Size (1980 - 1970)	0.0005	1.9
# Employees in		
High-Wage Manufacturing (1970)	0.0002	0.6
High-Wage Services (1970)	-0.0002	-0.5
Low-Wage Manufacturing (1970)	-0.0014	-1.7
Low-Wage Services (1970)	-2.59E-5	-0.0
Change in # Employees:		
High-Wage Manufacturing (1978 - 1970)	0.0008	1.8
High-Wage Services (1978 - 1970)	-6.73E-6	-0.0
Low-Wage Manufacturing (1978 - 1970)	-0.0011	-0.9
Low-Wage Services (1978 - 1970)	0.0005	0.8
High-Wage Manufacturing Dummy	-3.6431	-1.8
Distance from Interstate Highway	-0.0331	-0.6
Median Value of Home	-0.0002	-2.7
Percentage of Employees in		
HQ Firms in LMA (1970)	0.7657	5.7
Percentage in 1970:		
Females in Work Force	-0.6537	-2.5
Minority Population	-0.3075	-1.5
Elderly Population	0.1471	0.5
Percentage Change between 1970 and 1980:		
Females in Work Force	0.5448	13.6
Minority Population	-0.0005	-0.2
Elderly Population	0.2722	6.5
Population Size x Percentage Change of		
Females in Work Force	-5.16E-6	-3.7

$F = 34.857$, $df = 23$, 618, $p < 0.0001$; $R^2 = 0.56$; adjusted $R^2 = 0.55$

inequality due to the differential location of low- and high-paying service industries among communities with respect to population size.

Another major finding is the positive impact of increasing numbers of females in the community labor force on the position of the community in the income hierarchy. Increasing employment opportunities for females tend to lead to gains in aggregate income for the community, relative to other places. The interaction between population size and percentage gain of females in the work force suggests that the smallest communities experienced the greatest benefits from increasing female labor force participation.

The strength of the effect declines with increasing population size to the extent that the largest places underwent a loss in their rank position as gains in female labor force participation increased. This negative effect is most likely due to the large-scale job losses in high-wage manufacturing occurring in these places. In addition, larger gains in the elderly population had a positive impact on the community's position. This point will be returned to shortly.

The importance of gains in the female work force leads one to ask about the community factors that result in such an increase. Table 4.11 reports results from a regression analysis predicting percentage change in female work force participation as a function of the community variables described in the prior analysis.[28] As in the prior analysis, the OLS results are reported rather than those from the bounded influence regression since differences between the two are minimal.

Results indicate that female labor force participation increased as a function of decreasing manufacturing employment, implying that females entered the work force to compensate for lost jobs in manufacturing. Also, a larger percentage of elderly in the community promotes female labor force participation, most likely by promoting the development of various service industries, such as health care. Communities experiencing higher levels of percentage growth in minority population also saw greater gains in female work force participation; it is likely that higher levels of poverty and financial hardship among blacks and other minority groups force a larger proportion of women to enter the labor force, particularly in low-wage service sector jobs. In addition, a larger percentage of black households are headed by women.

However, places experiencing population growth, rather than decline, saw a larger percentage increase of females in the work force. Also, the smallest and very largest[29] communities experienced the biggest gains in female work force participation.

SUMMARY

This research indicates that disparities in the distribution of income across different-sized places widened over the 1970–80 decade, despite the greatest benefits from gains in the low-wage and high-wage service sectors accruing to rural communities. This trend is most likely a result of the tendency for higher-paying service jobs to locate in more urbanized areas.

Table 4.11
OLS Regression Analysis: Predicting Percentage Change in Female Work Force
Participation: 1979–1969

Variables	Estimate	t-value
Intercept	110.7535	12.6
Percentage of Females in Work Force (1970)	-2.8996	-12.7
Population Size (1970)	-0.0002	-4.8
Quadratic Effect: Population Size (1970)	2.53E-10	4.6
Change in Population Size (1980 - 1970)	0.0009	7.2
# Employees in		
High-Wage Manufacturing (1970)	-0.0002	-0.6
High-Wage Services (1970)	0.0006	1.5
Low-Wage Manufacturing (1970)	-0.0006	-1.1
Low-Wage Services (1970)	0.0008	1.0
Change in # Employees:		
High-Wage Manufacturing (1978 - 1970)	-0.0010	-2.3
High-Wage Manufacturing Dummy	-5.6822	-2.8
Distance from Interstate Highway	-0.0596	-1.2
Median Value of Home	0.0005	9.3
Percentage of Employees in		
HQ Firms in LMA (1970)	0.1197	0.9
Percentage in 1970:		
Minority Population	0.0640	0.3
Elderly Population	-0.0323	-0.1
Percentage Change between 1970 and 1980:		
Minority Population	0.0065	2.6
Elderly Population	0.5324	15.1

F = 61.203, df = 17, 624, $p < 0.0001$; R^2 = 0.62; adjusted R^2 = 0.61

However, results also emphasize the negative impact of an overdependence on manufacturing as a source of income. A strong service sector component to the community's industrial mix, in addition to manufacturing, provides greater economic stability for the community.

Communities experiencing an increase in rank are those with the capacity to integrate the contributions of less-dominant groups into the local economy, such as women or the elderly. An avenue through which these groups can become more active in the local economy is through the service sector.[30]

The downside is that the income potential of these service sector jobs does not appear to match that of jobs in manufacturing. As reported in the prior section, places with larger percentages of women in the work force experienced declines in aggregate income over the decade as the income distribution shifted to the lower end. That is, the number of families in the lower half of the distribution increased, while the number of families in the upper half decreased.

But by utilizing a greater proportion of the available work force, communities gain in terms of their share of income in the region, relative to other places. Income losses in high-wage manufacturing can be partially overridden by providing new avenues of employment; any sector that employs groups underrepresented in manufacturing, such as women, utilizes a greater proportion of the available work force. The potential of any industrial sector, including services, to induce multipliers in the local economy is enhanced by increasing the proportion of community members contributing to the local economy.

Hence, service sector growth indirectly benefits the community by providing the means for less dominant groups in the community to enter the local economy. The elderly contribute to this process by creating demand for service industries, such as health care.

NOTES

1. The median gain in (median) income for families was $1,683 (in 1982 constant dollars). Median income among families in the United States also increased over the decade, although the gain for communities in the sample is somewhat greater than that reported for all families in the Unites States. The U. S. Census reported that median family money income went from $25,248 in 1969 to $26,215 in 1979 (in 1982 constant dollars) (U.S. Bureau of the Census, 1980: Table 753; 1981: Table 726).

2. Total change is decomposed into four components: (1) change in the mean, (2) change in dispersion or variance, (3) change in relative or position or rank ordering of each community, and (4) change in the combined effect of position and dispersion (Collver and Semyonov, 1979: 483–84). Collver and Semyonov (1979: 484–85) use the magnitude and sign of the fourth component to indicate whether distances across communities increased or decreased over a period of time.

Two major sources of change were positional or ranked change, accounting for 63.8 percent of total change, and change in dispersion, accounting for 36 percent.

3. Note that these changes are relative, since the percentage of families in the middle of the income distribution is considerably greater than the percentage of families in the lower and upper tiers. Even among communities moving towards a bifurcated income distribution, the percentage of families in 1979 located in the middle tier of the income distribution, on average, was 60 percent, while the average percentage of families in the lower and upper tiers was 17 percent and 23 percent, respectively.

4. In 38 communities (5.9 percent of the total), the percentage of families in the middle increased rather than decreased.

5. Change between 1969 and 1979 is defined as the difference in mean percentages for these two years (1979–1969).

6. Refer to Table 3.2 for a list of industries classified as part of the low-wage and high-wage sectors.

7. Table 3.1 reports the endpoints (in 1982 constant dollars) for each income group.

8. The specific procedure is implemented through weighted least squares (WLS). Observations are downweighted to the extent that the residual or leverage of the case, obtained from ordinary least squares, exceeds a criterion (Belsley et al., 1980:274; Kassab, 1990c; Sheather and Hettmansperger, 1987). Refer to Appendix G for a more detailed discussion of the procedure.

9. The bootstrap involves repeatedly sampling, with replacement, residuals from the robust regression; this procedure is repeated about 1,056 times, thereby creating 1,056 bootstrap samples. Regression coefficients for the model are estimated for each bootstrap sample. The variance for each regression coefficient is calculated from the coefficients obtained from bootstrap samples (Efron and Gong, 1983:43).

10. The series of regression analyses is limited because each regression model constitutes an analysis independent of the others. This means that results from these models do not indicate whether changes in the different income groups occur together. To correct for this, a canonical correlation analysis was conducted in order to determine the combination of income groups associated with changes in the industrial sectors.

11. Bootstrapped standard errors were used in the calculation of asymptotic z-values.

12. These statistics are from the ordinary least squares (OLS) models. Because the bounded influence regression estimates in tables 4.4 and 4.5 are WLS estimates, goodness-of-fit statistics such as R^2 do not have a direct interpretation (Aldrich and Nelson, 1984:14–15).

13. Collinearity diagnostics indicate the presence of moderate linear dependencies in the data; condition numbers range between 23 and 28 for the OLS models and between 14 and 21 for the robust models. However, these linear dependencies primarily affect the precision of variables measuring population size, as indicated by analyses of the various inflation factors and the decomposition of the variances for the regression coefficients (Belsley et al., 1980: 112–17).

14. The canonical correlation analysis between change in the number of families in each income group and change in each industrial sector is based on partial correlation coefficients (SAS Institute, Inc., 1985:143). Variables partialed out of the analysis include all population size and change variables, as well as all other control variables included in the regression models. The 1970 level of each industrial variable is also partialed out of the correlations, since the intent is to examine the impact of *changes* in industrial mix on the income distribution. Interactions involving industrial change variables are not included in order to reduce the complexity of the analysis. The effect of outliers is taken into account by using the same weighting system as used in the analysis of change in aggregate income, described in Appendix G. Hence, the results from the canonical correlation analysis are considered robust.

The likelihood ratio tests indicate that three pairs of canonical variates are statistically significant ($F = 7.352$, $df = 24$, 2143.2; $F = 5.1389$, $df = 15$, 1698.15; $F = 3.9572$, $df = 8$, 1232; $p<.0001$ for all three variates). Canonical correlations are 0.36, 0.24, and 0.20; the respective eigenvalues for the canonical variates accounted for 56.6 percent, 25.6 percent, and 14.9 percent of the variance.

15. The standardized and raw canonical coefficients for the first three variates, as reported in Table 4.9, are the weights in the linear combination of standardized variables,

(that is, mean of zero and variance of one). Raw coefficients are the weights used in the linear combination of unstandardized variables (SAS Institute Inc., 1985:145).

16. The sign of the coefficient for low-wage services switches from negative to positive when communities have approximately 2,850 employees in the sector in 1970; places with at least this many workers in the sector represent about 10 percent of the sample.

17. The expansion of the lower-middle income group as a result of increased employment in low-wage services in these places may be due to an increase in the number of families with multiple wage earners or individual job holders with multiple jobs. For instance, the proportion of families with multiple wage earners has been increasing at a fairly steady rate since the early 1950s (Hayghe, 1990: Chart 1). The increased number of new jobs in this sector could provide the opportunity for multiple job-holding to occur.

18. These results suggest the presence of an interaction between employment change in low-wage services and low-wage manufacturing, since growth in both these sectors results in gains to the lower-middle income group. The multiplier effect from growth in low-wage manufacturing would be sufficient to spur development of lower-level services, such as convenience stores and other retail industries. But smaller communities or those in more remote locations have a greater propensity to experience growth in low-wage manufacturing employment ($r = -0.25, p < .0001$ and $r = 0.11, p < .01$, respectively).

Perhaps the reason high-wage services are not involved in the effect is that the combination of growth in these two lower-paying sectors does not provide the community with enough financial resources or human capital to attract services associated with the higher paying producer service sector. This is a likely scenario for rural communities, since other factors attracting higher-level firms are limited.

19. In support of this contention, communities with diversified local economies tend to be larger in population size ($r = 0.18, p < .0001$) and more centrally located ($r = 0.13, p < .001$).

20. The values graphed in Figure 4.2 are taken from Table 4.7a, while the values for Figure 4.3 are from Tables 4.8a, 4.8b, and 4.8d.

21. Table H.1 in Appendix H reports average characteristics of communities when grouped by remoteness of location.

22. Refer to Table H.2 in Appendix H for a cross-classification of growth in low-wage and high-wage service sector by population size; a summary of the results is provided.

23. The median number of jobs lost in high-wage manufacturing among places located on the interstate highway is 147, nearly eight times the median number lost by any other place, when grouped by distance from an interstate highway. The median number of jobs lost in low-wage manufacturing among centrally located places is 36; this is more than three times the median amount lost by any other place (refer to Table H.1 in Appendix H).

24. Preliminary analyses indicated that some coefficients were being distorted when this term was absent from the model. Stepwise regression aided in determining which interaction term was needed to correct the distortion.

25. Supplemental analyses indicated that communities with diversified industrial structures are better able to adjust for job losses in a given sector, as evidenced by the tendency for these places to experience gains in position in the hierarchy.

26. Robust estimates for the point at which communities would decline in rank is 300,000; this estimate differs somewhat from that derived from OLS estimates.

27. Table H.2 in Appendix H reveals that this relationship holds for places in this sample also.

28. The model presented in Table 4.11 is a reduced model, meaning terms that were clearly nonsignificant were deleted from the model. The initial model contained variables measuring employment change in both service sectors and low-wage manufacturing, as well as interaction terms between employment variables and community remoteness.

29. Robust estimates indicate that communities over 300,000 would experience gains in rank.

30. The correlation between percentage change in females in the work force and whether the community has a service-based economy is 0.11, $p < .01$.

5

A National Study of the Impact of Service Sector Employment on Wages: Rural and Urban Counties During the 1980s

This chapter reports results from analyses using recent data for all counties in the United States and the District of Columbia. The impact of the changing structure of employment on aggregate wages and salary disbursements in the county is examined with income and employment data from the 1978–1988 period. A two-wave panel study is used to determine whether results obtained for low-wage and high-wage service sectors in the Mid-Atlantic region during the 1970s continued through the 1980s, and whether these results generalize to the United States as a whole. Also, employment in low-wage and high-wage service sectors is disaggregated in order to determine which industries have the largest impact on aggregate wages and salaries. Employment data is from County Business Patterns (CBP), while data on income and population are from the Bureau of Economic Analysis (BEA).

The models presented in this chapter are analogous to those discussed in the prior chapter. Variables central to the analysis are change in the level of employment in various manufacturing and service sector industries between 1978 and 1987. Again, change in employment levels is measured by calculating the difference in the number of employees for each sector between the two years (1987–1978). In the first model presented in this chapter, the service sector is broken into low-wage and high-wage sectors. The second model disaggregates low-wage and high-wage services into their major components, as defined by the two-digit (1972) SIC codes.

Also, both models include the 1978 level of employment in each industrial sector in order to control for the initial predominance of a particular sector on wages and salaries. Population size in 1979, its quadratic effect, population change between 1979 and 1988, and the interaction between 1979 population size and change are included in order to control the association between population size and change in aggregate wages and salaries in the county. Specific reasons for including each of these terms are presented in the third chapter.

Some differences exist between the models discussed here and in the prior chapter, however. The dependent variable in this chapter is change in wage and salary disbursements between 1979 and 1988 (in 1982–84 constant dollars), rather than family income.[1] To capture differences in effects between rural and urban places, separate regressions are run here for metropolitan and nonmetropolitan areas. The measure of remoteness used in the prior chapter, distance from an interstate highway, was not readily available for this data set. Also, variables controlling on demographic changes in the county, such as female work force participation, are not included in the model here, since data from the 100 percent count of the 1990 U.S. census is still preliminary, with much of the data not yet available.

Another difference from the prior chapter is that the low-wage and high-wage manufacturing sectors are collapsed into a single category. The analyses in the prior chapter indicated that differences between the two sectors in effects on income and income distribution are minor within both rural areas and urban areas. By collapsing the two manufacturing categories, the potential for missing data is also reduced because data might be reported for one category and not the other, and the analysis is simplified.

IMPACT OF SERVICE AND MANUFACTURING EMPLOYMENT ON WAGES AND SALARIES: 1978–1988

Table 5.1 contains results from the regression models examining the impact of changing employment structures on wages and salaries in metropolitan and nonmetropolitan areas. The industry variables measuring change in employment are essentially not affected by outliers. Because conclusions do not differ between OLS and robust regressions for these variables, which are the focus of the study, OLS results are reported.[2]

Both models are statistically significant, with the nonmetropolitan and metropolitan models accounting for 67 percent and 95 percent of the variance in the dependent variable, respectively.[3] The reason the R^2s are so high is because of the high correlation between population size (as well as change in population size) and change in aggregate wages and salaries. For the nonmetropolitan model, the correlations of 1979 population size and change in population with change in wages and salaries are 0.26 and 0.64, respectively; corresponding correlation coefficients for the metropolitan model are 0.65 and 0.69.

Table 5.1
OLS Regression Analyses for Nonmetropolitan and Metropolitan Counties: Predicting Change in Aggregate Wage and Salary Disbursements: 1988-1979

Variables	Nonmetropolitan Estimate	t-value	Metropolitan Estimate	t-value
Intercept	4842.78	4.7	33140.79	2.1
Population Size (1979)	-104.392	-11.2	-61.81336	-4.5
Quadratic Effect: Population Size (1979)	0.05120	7.4	0.001759	8.1
Change in Population Size (1988 - 1979)	216.604	7.7	-0.442365	-0.0
Population Size (1979) x Change in Population	-0.00376	-0.1	-0.005708	-4.6
# Employees in				
Manufacturing (1978)	3.98620	12.4	1.969449	2.1
Low-Wage Services (1978)	-5.80344	-5.6	-32.08130	-14.8
High-Wage Services (1978)	3.11251	3.8	16.47240	27.0
Change in # Employees:				
Manufacturing (1987 - 1978)	16.98755	22.6	31.87698	14.9
Low-Wage Services (1987 - 1978)	25.61208	18.5	30.43176	7.8
High-Wage Services (1987 - 1978)	13.46648	13.2	37.28465	21.4
F-value:	460.305		1403.223	
df =	10, 2282		10, 708	
R^2 =	0.67		0.95	
adjusted R^2 =	0.67		0.95	

The regression coefficients for nonmetropolitan counties indicate that a new job in low-wage services is worth about $26,000. The effect of low-wage service sector growth is significantly greater than the effect of growth in manufacturing or high-wage services ($F = 27.2563$, $df = 1, 2,282$, $p < 0.001$; $F = 38.8589$, $df = 1, 2,282$, $p < 0.001$, respectively). A new job in manufacturing or high-wage services is worth about $17,000 or $13,500 in aggregate wages and salaries, respectively, to the nonmetropolitan county.

These findings support statements made in the previous chapter regarding the positive impact of the low-wage service sector on the nonmetropolitan economy, and the fact that growth in this sector represents a potential source of economic development. The positive effect of low-wage services appears to have continued throughout the 1980s despite declines in manufacturing employment in nonmetropolitan counties.

The small magnitude of the estimated coefficients for manufacturing and high-wage services in nonmetropolitan counties compared to metropolitan counties is notable.[4] This implies that income derived from jobs in manufacturing and high-wage services does not have the income potential in rural areas as in urban areas.

Most likely, the magnitude for manufacturing in nonmetropolitan counties is partially suppressed due to conflicting trends in manufacturing employment: over 50 percent of the nonmetropolitan counties experienced a decrease in manufacturing employment, while the remainder saw some gains.[5] The estimated coefficient for high-wage services in rural areas may be smaller than expected because of the preponderance of part-time employment in this sector and the growth of lower-level occupations in this sector (that is, the growth of "back office" activities) (Glasmeier and Borchard, 1989). This latter idea will be discussed again shortly.

Among metropolitan areas, the high-wage service sector is a major contributor to the economy, having an estimated impact on income that is at least as great as manufacturing. A new job in high-wage services is estimated to be worth about $37,000 to the county. Increasing employment in manufacturing or low-wage services also has a positive impact on aggregate income. The estimated coefficients indicate that a new job in manufacturing leads to an additional $31,900 in aggregate wages and salaries in the county, while a new job in low-wage services is estimated to be worth about $30,500. However, the estimated effect of high-wage services does not appear to differ significantly from the estimated effect of either manufacturing or low-wage services ($z = 1.65$, $p < 0.10$; $z = 1.37$, $p < 0.18$, respectively, using the z-test for the difference between two correlated random variables).[6]

Recall that during the 1970s low-wage service sector growth was associated with decline in aggregate income among centrally located places in the Mid-Atlantic region. This contrasts sharply with the positive effect of growth in that sector during the 1980s. It appears that the positive impact of growth in low-wage services during the 1970s was suppressed due to extreme employment losses in manufacturing.

In order to better explicate those service industries likely to make a contribution to the county economy, the low-wage and high-wage service sectors were disaggregated into functional components, with the 1972 two-digit SIC code used to classify the data. The revised regression model is presented in Tables 5.2a and 5.2b. In this model, the various industries comprising the low-wage and high-wage service sectors are entered as separate variables. The low-wage sector is comprised of retail trade and personal services, while all other components are classified as part of the high-wage sector.[7]

Both models are statistically significant; the R^2 for the nonmetropolitan model is 0.71 ($F = 218.753$, $df = 22, 1991$, $p < 0.001$), while the R^2 for the metropolitan model is 0.975 ($F = 1255.220$, $df = 22, 690$, $p < 0.001$).[8] Again, the R^2 values for the regression models are high due to the high correlations of population size and population change with change in aggregate wage and salary disbursements.

In Table 5.2a, robust estimates from the bounded influence regression models are reported, due to the impact of outliers on estimates for some of the variables measuring employment change in a sector.[9] The standard errors for the models were bootstrapped using the procedure described in Appendix G. In Table 5.2b, the standardized regression coefficients are reported in order to compare the relative importance of the various service industries included in the regression.

For nonmetropolitan counties, the positive impact of increasing employment in business and professional services, as well as retail trade, is readily apparent (refer to Table 5.1a). The estimated effects for growth in retail trade and business/professional services are significantly greater than the effect of manufacturing growth on aggregate wages (retail trade: $z = 4.22$; business/professional: $z = 4.53$, $p < 0.01$ for both tests, using the z-test for the difference between two correlated random variables).

In addition, the impact of a new job in either retail trade or business/professional services exceeds that of a new job in wholesale trade, or finance, insurance, and real estate (FIRE). Differences between business/professional services and both wholesale trade and FIRE are statistically significant (FIRE: $z = 2.86$, $p < 0.01$; wholesale trade: $z = 2.34$, $p < 0.02$), while for retail trade differences are weaker but still marginally significant (FIRE: $z = 2.00$, $p < 0.05$; wholesale trade: $z = 1.41$, $p < 0.20$).

An important implication of these results is that even though retail trade is a part of the low-wage service sector, its impact on wages in nonmetropolitan counties compares favorably with manufacturing and the higher-paying producer service industries. This positive effect is most likely due to import substitution, and the export potential of retail trade in places with substantial proportions of the population relying on income from extralocal sources, such as pensions or Social Security (Gillis, 1987; Marquand, 1979).

Employment growth in manufacturing and retail trade are the most important predictors of increasing wage and salary disbursements in nonmetropolitan counties (refer to Table 5.2b). While business/professional services appear to be an

Table 5.2
Robust Regression Analyses for Nonmetropolitan and Metropolitan Counties:
Predicting Change in Aggregate Wage and Salary Disbursements: 1988–1979

Panel a: Regression Coefficients and Asymptotic Z-Values

Variables	Nonmetropolitan Estimate	Nonmetropolitan z-value	Metropolitan Estimate	Metropolitan z-value
Intercept	3606.78	3.0	-8758.61	-0.6
Population Size (1979)	-70.2172	-6.6	84.9802	4.4
Quadratic Effect: Population Size (1979)	0.02378	3.2	0.00012	0.5
Change in Population Size (1988 - 1979)	198.070	6.9	-85.5181	-1.8
Population Size (1979) x Change in Population	0.07022	1.9	0.00138	1.0
# Employees in				
Manufacturing (1978)	3.75784	11.6	1.71020	1.8
Transportation, Communications, and Public Utilities (TCU) (1978)	-13.8168	-4.9	-7.47798	-2.1
Wholesale Trade (1978)	-0.17879	-0.1	-3.53697	-0.7
Finance, Insurance, and Real Estate (FIRE) (1978)	7.02955	1.8	20.1402	5.4
Business and Professional Service (1978)	3.65349	1.2	11.5812	2.0
Medical and Health Services (1978)	6.44562	2.9	-14.5740	-2.2
Social Services (1978)	12.21438	5.1	40.5421	7.5
Retail Trade (1978)	-6.76817	-3.8	-23.8251	-7.3
Personal Services (1978)	1.38190	0.6	2.09487	0.4
Change in # Employees:				
Manufacturing (1987 - 1978)	15.47727	20.3	28.02600	13.8
Transportation, Communications, and Public Utilities (TCU) (1987 - 1978)	3.58725	1.4	10.72001	2.2
Wholesale Trade (1987 - 1978)	18.3426	4.4	53.84133	7.9
Finance, Insurance, and Real Estate (FIRE) (1987 - 1978)	15.0561	3.7	46.75464	9.1
Business and Professional Services (1987 - 1978)	31.2844	9.2	39.91582	8.1
Medical and Health Services (1987 - 1978)	2.16476	0.7	11.49634	1.2
Social Services (1987 - 1978)	8.28201	3.9	-17.29060	-2.0
Retail Trade (1987 - 1978)	25.1129	12.2	22.95502	4.0
Personal Services (1987 - 1978)	8.25948	2.4	18.77690	3.7

Percentage (Number) of Cases Downweighted: 8.3 (167)   9.4 (67)

Panel b: Standardized Regression Coefficients

Variables	Nonmetropolitan Estimate	Metropolitan Estimate
Population Size (1979)	-0.4014	0.2824
Quadratic Effect: Population Size (1979)	0.1221	0.0070
Change in Population Size (1988 - 1979)	0.2079	-0.0522
Population Size (1979) x Change in Population	0.0452	0.0108
# Employees in		
Manufacturing (1978)	0.2928	0.0630
Transportation, Communications, and Public Utilities (TCU) (1978)	-0.1334	-0.0654
Wholesale Trade (1978)	-0.0018	-0.0332
Finance, Insurance, and Real Estate (FIRE) (1978)	0.0527	0.1970
Business and Professional Service (1978)	0.0171	0.0990
Medical and Health Services (1978)	0.0813	-0.1282
Social Services (1978)	0.0855	0.1832
Retail Trade (1978)	-0.2363	-0.5448
Personal Services (1978)	0.0143	0.0139

Table 5.2 continued

Change in # Employees:		
Manufacturing (1987 - 1978)	0.3481	0.3019
Transportation, Communications, and Public Utilities (TCU) (1987 - 1978)	0.0212	0.0335
Wholesale Trade (1987 - 1978)	0.0782	0.1885
Finance, Insurance, and Real Estate (FIRE) (1987 - 1978)	0.0619	0.2114
Business and Professional Services (1987 - 1978)	0.1659	0.3267
Medical and Health Services (1987 - 1978)	0.0148	0.0501
Social Services (1987 - 1978)	0.0534	-0.0428
Retail Trade (1987 - 1978)	0.3473	0.1765
Personal Services (1987 - 1978)	0.0442	0.0533

important contributor to the nonmetropolitan economy, their importance is considerably less than either retail trade or manufacturing. The tendency for firms in this sector to locate in metropolitan counties probably reduces the importance of these firms being a means for achieving economic growth and development in nonmetropolitan areas.[10]

In metropolitan counties, the employment market is considerably more varied than in nonmetropolitan counties, with jobs in manufacturing, business/professional services, FIRE, wholesale trade, and retail trade all constituting important contributors to the metropolitan economy.[11]

Further, the impact of a new job in wholesale trade, FIRE, or business/professional services on wage and salary disbursements is significantly greater than that associated with a new job in manufacturing ($z = 3.33, p < 0.001; z = 3.41, p < 0.001; z = 2.14, p < 0.05$, respectively, using the z-test for the difference between two correlated random variables). In contrast, the difference in estimated effects between manufacturing and retail trade is not substantial.[12] However, the positive effect of manufacturing on wages is considerably more consistent than any of the effects stemming from growth in the service sector, in the sense that its z-value is significantly greater.

Employment gains in transportation, communication, and public utilities (TCPU) and personal services also have a positive effect on aggregate wages and salaries in the county. However, neither TCPU nor personal services is a major predictor of aggregate wages and salaries, based on their small standardized coefficients.

Surprisingly, increasing employment in social services is associated with a decline in wage and salary disbursements. The negative effect may be a result of social service employment growing in response to a large population who is indigent or experiencing financial hardship. In contrast, the effect of increasing employment in social services in nonmetropolitan counties is positive. It is likely that the introduction of a new source of employment in any industry in nonmetropolitan America will have a positive effect on the local economy due to a shortage of jobs. Moreover, the human services provided by this sector, such as adult education or day care, help promote a more equitable distribution of benefits by aiming benefits to groups with the greatest need (Couto, 1990).

It is important to note that among nonmetropolitan counties, the impact on wage and salary disbursements of introducing a new job in a particular sector tends to be smaller than the corresponding effect in metropolitan counties, based on the magnitudes of the regression coefficients. For example, in metropolitan counties, the positive effects of increasing employment in manufacturing, wholesale trade, and FIRE are significantly greater than the corresponding effects in nonmetropolitan counties ($z = 5.78, 4.45, 4.81$, respectively, $p < 0.001$ for all three tests, using the z-test for two independent samples). The implication is that jobs in nonmetropolitan counties tend to be lower-paying ones.

One reason for the discrepancies between nonmetropolitan and metropolitan counties could be that large firms are moving many of their "back office" functions to rural areas, where the cost of living and the cost of labor are considerably less than in highly urbanized areas. These jobs are lower-level and consequently lower-paying positions, such as data entry services (Glasmeier and Borchard, 1989:1578).[13] Conversely, higher level, and consequently higher paying, "front office" activities continue to centralize in urban areas. Work by Porterfield and Kassab (1991) looks in greater detail at the types of producer service growing in rural areas and the contribution of back office activities to that growth.

RURAL AND URBAN WAGE DIFFERENCES: SERVICES AND MANUFACTURING INDUSTRIES

In the next analysis, the gap in wages in manufacturing and producer service industries between rural and urban areas is scrutinized more closely by comparing the payroll of various industries across metropolitan and nonmetropolitan counties. In Figure 5.1, average yearly wages in 1987 (in 1982–84 constant dollars) for various service industries and manufacturing are plotted separately for nonmetropolitan and metropolitan counties. Specifically, these figures represent total first-quarter payroll in each sector, multiplied by four and divided by the number of employees in that sector, as of mid-March. Data are from the County Business Patterns.

The graph clearly portrays the difference in yearly wages expected between metropolitan and nonmetropolitan counties among manufacturing and service industries: average yearly wages in nonmetropolitan counties are consistently lower than in metropolitan counties. Nonmetropolitan wages in retail trade come closest to meeting metropolitan wages, although some gap still remains.

It is evident from Figure 5.1 and the analyses described above that manufacturing and most of the service industries are sensitive to the hierarchical arrangement of places, meaning that lower-paying positions tend to locate in nonmetropolitan areas. The largest difference in wages between nonmetropolitan and metropolitan counties is found in manufacturing. However, several industries in the higher-

Figure 5.1
Comparison of Nonmetropolitan and Metropolitan Average Yearly Wages

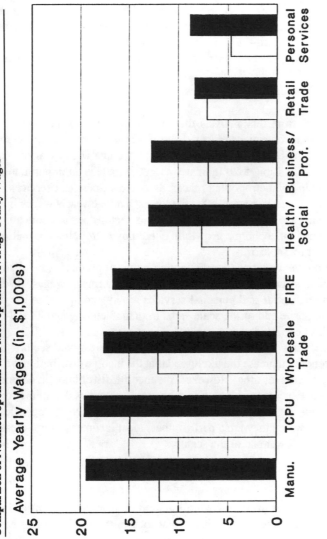

Average Yearly Wages (in $1,000s)

Manu. TCPU Wholesale FIRE Health/ Business/ Retail Personal
Trade Social Prof. Trade Services

☐ Nonmetropolitan ■ Metropolitan

Metropolitan sample size is 719 or 720 counties, and the nonmetropolitan sample ranges
from 2,295 to 2,353 counties.

paying producer services, such as business/professional services, also evidence large differences in yearly wages between metropolitan and nonmetropolitan counties.

Within nonmetropolitan counties, average yearly wages in manufacturing tend to be about the same as those in wholesale trade and FIRE. Yearly wages in manufacturing are somewhat higher than in business/professional services, health[14] and social services, or retail trade. In general, however, these service industries have a large proportion of part-time employees compared with manufacturing (Appelbaum and Albin, 1990: Table 3.7; Stanback and Noyelle, 1982), resulting in accentuated differences in yearly wages. It is likely that discrepancies in hourly rates are smaller.

It is also evident from this analysis that, in nonmetropolitan counties, retail trade, which is part of consumer services, is fairly similar to business/professional services and health and social services in terms of average yearly wages. Recall that results reported in Table 5.2b indicate that retail trade is an important determinant of income in nonmetropolitan places. In contrast, personal services, also part of the consumer service sector, offer the lowest average yearly wages in nonmetropolitan counties. Employment growth in this sector does not constitute an important component of economic growth in either nonmetropolitan or metropolitan counties (refer to Table 5.2).

Within metropolitan counties, the distinction between producer (and distributive) services and consumer services appears to hold in terms of wages. Average yearly wages in retail trade and personal services are low compared to the other sectors. At the opposite end of the scale, jobs in manufacturing and TCPU offer some of the highest expected yearly wages.

Large disparities in wages between the highest- and lowest-paid sectors in the metropolitan economy increase the likelihood that the income distribution will become more bifurcated over time. However, the income distribution in nonmetropolitan areas is not expected to bipolarize to the same extent as that in metropolitan areas, since jobs locating in rural areas tend to be lower-paying, regardless of industrial sector of which they are a part. Rather, most incomes in rural areas are expected to be at the lower end of the scale.

SUMMARY

Results from analyses of nonmetropolitan and metropolitan counties in the United States from 1978 to 1988 indicate that jobs in the service sector have a positive impact on aggregate wages and salaries. In metropolitan areas, jobs in business services are at least as important as manufacturing in promoting gains in wage and salary disbursements. Employment growth in FIRE, wholesale trade, and retail trade is also an important predictor of increased earnings.

Compared to the producer and distributive services, consumer services tend to have smaller effects on aggregate wages and salaries. Whether the incomes of metropolitan workers will invariably be reduced due to the prevalence of employment in low-wage services is uncertain. While average yearly earnings in these service industries are less than in manufacturing or producer services, workers are increasingly holding multiple jobs in order to obtain a higher standard of living.[15]

In nonmetropolitan counties manufacturing continues to be a major source of growth in wages, along with retail trade. Reducing the proportion of jobs in manufacturing would reduce aggregate wages and salaries because the only service sector providing a major contribution to the nonmetropolitan economy is retail trade. Developing jobs in wholesale trade and FIRE could help offset losses in manufacturing, since average yearly wages are as high in these two service industries as they are in manufacturing among nonmetropolitan counties.[16] In addition, a nonmetropolitan economy might benefit from a diversification of its economic base. However, at present, neither wholesale trade nor FIRE is an important part of most nonmetropolitan counties.

Developing retail trade, health, and social services in nonmetropolitan economies has potential in terms of employment as well. However, the high rate of part-time employment in these sectors (Appelbaum and Albin, 1990: Table 3.7) implies that a traditional family wage can be achieved only if a worker holds more than one job or if multiple members of the household work in part-time or full-time employment.

NOTES

1. 1979 was a peak year for the U.S. economy as a whole, while 1988 was close to the peak that occurred in 1989. The Consumer Price Index with a 1982–84 base is the basis for making the conversion to constant dollars.

2. Outliers in the data affected primarily those variables measuring the impact of population size, particularly in the metropolitan counties model. Also, the variable estimating the effect of 1978 level of employment in high-wage services is overestimated by OLS. Because coefficients and standard errors for all other industry variables are highly similar, the OLS results are reported in Table 5.1. As discussed in Appendix G, OLS results are preferred over those from the robust regression when differences between the two are minor.

Also, collinearity diagnostics indicate that intercorrelations among the independent variables do not have a detrimental effect on the stability of regression coefficients in the model.

3. Industries excluded from the analysis include agriculture, mining, construction, membership organizations, and government. Data on government, agriculture production, railroad, and household employment are not available through County Business Patterns (U.S. Bureau of the Census, 1982b). Other sectors were excluded from the model because unstable estimates of their impact were produced in some populations, for example, the effect of agriculture in metropolitan counties.

4. Differences in the regression coefficients between nonmetropolitan and metropolitan counties for manufacturing and high-wage services are statistically significant ($z = -6.56$ and -11.78, respectively, $p < 0.001$ for all three tests, using the z-test for two independent samples). The effect of increased employment in low-wage services does not

appear to differ between nonmetropolitan and metropolitan counties ($z = -1.16$, $p <$ 0.25).

5. Descriptive statistics for variables in the nonmetropolitan and metropolitan models are presented in Table H.3 in Appendix H.

6. The lack of significance is most likely due to variation among metropolitan counties in terms of their industrial or employment base.

7. Two-digit 1972 SIC codes are used to define components of the high-wage service sector as follows: transportation, communication, and public utilities (40–42, 44–49), wholesale trade (50, 51), finance, insurance and real estate (60–67), business and professional services (73, 81, 89), medical and health services (80), and social services (82–84). Components of the low-wage service sector are defined as follows: retail trade (52–59), personal service (75–79).

Membership organizations (SIC code 86) were excluded from the analysis due to instability in the regression coefficients resulting from a change in procedures for collecting employment data on nonprofit organizations between 1978 and 1987. Firms with a 2-digit SIC code of 84 (museums, botanical, and zoological gardens) are included as part of the low-wage sector in Table 5.1, but are were classified as a social service in the more detailed analysis of service industries. Error induced from this cross-coding is likely to be minimal due to the small number of employees in this category.

8. Collinearity diagnostics indicate that in the regression of metropolitan counties, regression coefficients for the population size variables and employment in low-wage services (in 1978) are affected by intercorrelations among the independent variables. However, none of the regression coefficients for variables measuring change in employment is detrimentally affected by multicollinearity.

9. The regression coefficients for finance, insurance, and real estate (FIRE) and social services in metropolitan counties are affected by outliers. The change in procedures for collecting employment data on nonprofit organizations between 1978 and 1987 contributed to the presence of outliers in variables measuring employment in social services.

10. Metropolitan counties are more likely than nonmetropolitan counties to experience employment growth in all of the service industries studied in this analysis ($r = 0.14$ for TCPU, 0.24 for wholesale trade, 0.41 for retail trade, 0.25 for FIRE, 0.31 for business/professional services, 0.41 for medical and health services, 0.27 for personal services, and 0.32 for social services; $p < 0.001$ for all Pearson product moment correlation coefficients).

11. The importance of retail trade to metropolitan economies supports the contention that the negative impact of growth in low-wage services on income during the 1970s was transitory.

12. Based on the z-test for the difference between two correlated random variables, the effect of growth in retail trade is smaller than these higher-paying services, and results are generally statistically significant (wholesale trade: $z = 3.29$, $p < 0.001$; FIRE: $z = 2.90$, $p < 0.01$; business/professional: $z = 1.87$, $p < 0.10$). However, the difference between the effect of growth in retail trade does not differ significantly from the effect of growth in personal services ($z = 0.51$, $p < 0.65$).

13. But only those rural places well-articulated with metropolitan areas in terms of transportation, communication, and telecommunications are likely to experience growth in back office facilities (Glasmeier and Borchard, 1989:1577–578).

14. The impact of increasing employment in medical and health services is not significant in either the nonmetropolitan or metropolitan sample. This represents an anomaly,

since the sector has shown fairly strong growth during the 1980s, relative to other sectors (see Table H.3). The lack of a significant effect may be due to collapsing a diverse array of industries into a single category; for example, average pay in nursing homes is low, while median pay among hospitals is high, among both part-time and full-time employees (Porterfield, 1990; Applebaum and Albin, 1990). Also, employment in the higher-paying hospital industry declined over the decade as federal contribution for hospital care of the elderly and poor declined. The other health industries with fairly low average pay scale were growing and provided 7.7 percent of new jobs in the economy (Appelbaum and Albin, 1990). Grouping these two types of health industries probably resulted in the effect for medical and health services being suppressed.

15. The proportion of jobholders with more than one job reached 6.2 percent in 1989, the highest level in more than 30 years (U.S. Department of Labor, 1989). Similarly, the proportion of families with multiple wage earners has been increasing at a fairly steady rate since the early 1950s (Hayghe, 1990: Chart 1). For instance, the percentage of families with at least two wage earners was 46 percent in 1980 but 50 percent in 1988 (U.S. Bureau of the Census, 1990: Table 672).

16. The positive impact of wholesale trade and FIRE on wage and salary disbursements was found to be less than retail trade in nonmetropolitan counties; this may be due to the inhibitory effect of employment losses in manufacturing employment during the 1980s, or job growth in the sector being represented by a large proportion of lower, part-time jobs.

6

Summary, Conclusions, and Policy Implications

In this chapter, results from the empirical analyses in the previous chapters are reviewed within the context of concerns about the effects of service sector growth. Also, implications of the results for economic development and social welfare policy are discussed.

SUMMARY AND SYNTHESIS OF FINDINGS

The research was motivated by several issues dealing with the ability of the service sector to maintain community income levels and promote the equitable distribution of income. One issue is whether jobs in the service sector can substitute for employment losses in manufacturing, which has been a source of middle-income jobs for large segments of the community work force. If sufficient levels of income can be derived from jobs in the service sector, the community as a whole will be able to retain past levels of aggregate income.

A second issue revolves around the impact of growth in both low-wage and high-wage services on the distribution of income in the community, and whether the distribution is becoming more inequitable over time. If the percentage of lower- and higher-income jobs increases while those in the middle decrease, barriers separating those in the lower income groups from the higher income brackets will become increasingly solidified.

A third issue focuses on the tendency for higher-paying producer and distributive services to locate predominately in urbanized areas; smaller or more remote places have experienced markedly less growth in the high-paying service sector. Since most employment growth is occurring in services, these differential location patterns may result in increasing inequities in the distribution of income across rural and urban places, as rural communities receive a smaller proportion of the total in the system.

The empirical analyses indicate that the impact of service sector growth on aggregate income levels depends on the remoteness of the community. Among rural places in the 1970s, growth in either low-wage or high-wage services led to increases in aggregate income. This trend continued during the 1980s. In particular, growth in retail trade appears to be a crucial element in the growth of the rural economy as a whole. Manufacturing also is an important component of overall growth in the rural community.

However, the impact of growth in the high-wage service sector during the 1980s among nonmetropolitan places was muted. This finding may be due to employment declines in rural manufacturing. Declining employment in manufacturing would lessen the demand for producer and distributive services connected with the manufacturing sector, resulting in a larger proportion of part-time jobs in these industries.

In contrast, among centrally located places in the 1970s, growth in low-wage services was associated with declines in aggregate income. Further, growth in high-wage services had a positive but smaller impact in centrally located places than in remotely located ones. It appears that income generated from these new service sector jobs was not sufficient to act as a substitute source of employment for jobs lost in manufacturing or other higher-paying sectors.

However, the impact of employment growth in the low-wage service sector reversed itself during the 1980s, and the positive effect of growth in high-wage services was magnified. Growth in both low-wage and high-wage services had a beneficial impact on community income, with the high-wage sector having the largest effect. Services most critical for achieving gains in aggregate wage and salary disbursements in metropolitan counties were finance, insurance, and real estate (FIRE), business services, wholesale trade, and retail trade. Retail trade is part of the low-wage sector, while the other critical service sectors are high-wage. Manufacturing was also an important contributor to economic growth in urban places.

In summary, results from the analysis indicate that growth in low-wage services has the capacity to add to the level of aggregate income in the community, with the effect being strongest among rural communities. Also, high-wage services appear to have the capacity to substitute, at least partially, for manufacturing as a source for maintaining aggregate income levels. However, in places where substantial declines in manufacturing have occurred, this ability is weakened. What appears evident over the two decades is that, in both rural and urban places, large declines in manufacturing are associated with the positive impact of growth in services being suppressed in the local economy.

Answers to the second concern, regarding the impact of the low- and high-wage service sectors on the distribution of income within the community, also depend on the remoteness of the community. Evidence from the 1970s supports the idea that service sector growth is associated with the income distribution becoming more bipolarized in centrally located places. Employment growth in high-wage services acts to increase the number of families in the highest income group, while growth in low-wage services results in an increase in the number of families in the lower half of the income distribution. As stated before, these places suffered from unusually large declines in manufacturing employment during this period.

Unfortunately, data on the distribution of income from the 1990 U.S. census is not yet available, so this idea is not examined here with more recent data. However, given results from the analysis of aggregate wages and salaries, I expect the service sector to have a less polarizing effect on the income distribution than in the 1970s, due to the development of alternative employment structures in services.

Among rural communities during the 1970s, service sector growth was associated with expansion of the middle income groups and contraction of the lower end of the income distribution. Growth in both low-wage and high-wage services acted to increase the number of families in the lower-middle and upper-middle groups, while it was associated with declines in the number of families in the lowest income group. As stated before, among remotely located places, growth in the middle of the income distribution occurred in conjunction with growth in manufacturing.

The third issue focuses on the tendency for high-paying producer services to locate in more urbanized places, and the impact of those trends on the distribution of income across communities within the region. Results indicate that increasing employment in the service sector does not directly affect the position of the community in the income hierarchy. Instead, results indicate that dependence on a declining economic sector, like high-wage branch manufacturing, was the primary industrial characteristic leading to a decrease in the community's position in the income hierarchy. The rank of these places tended to decrease, on average, by four positions over the decade.

Also, disparities in income levels between the smallest and more moderately sized places increased between 1969 and 1979.[1] Smaller communities underwent a redistribution of families toward the lower end of the income scale, while simultaneously experiencing a decrease in the level of aggregate resources and position in the urban hierarchy. However, income inequality increased within more moderately sized places as gains in aggregate income occurred. So during the 1970s, disparities between rural and urban places increased as the distribution of income within larger places also became more inequitable.

During the 1980s, wage differentials between rural and urban areas augmented preexisting discrepancies in availability of resources. The effect of growth in manufacturing is significantly lower in nonmetropolitan areas than in metropolitan areas, with average wage levels in nonmetropolitan counties considerably smaller than those in metropolitan ones. Also, average earnings in various high-paying services, such as FIRE and wholesale trade, are considerably lower in rural areas than in urban ones. Again, the effect of employment growth in these sectors on aggregate wages and salaries is significantly greater in metropolitan than non-metropolitan counties. In contrast, the difference between metropolitan and non-metropolitan average wage levels in retail trade is small.

While higher-paying producer and distributive service industries are not currently an important component of the nonmetropolitan economy, they have the same income potential as manufacturing. Among nonmetropolitan areas, average wages for wholesale trade and FIRE are as high as manufacturing. In addition, the differences between these service industries and retail trade are considerably smaller in nonmetropolitan counties than in metropolitan ones. By promoting the development of a variety of service industries in the local economy, including wholesale trade, FIRE, business services, and retail trade, gaps between rural and urban places have the potential to decrease.

IMPLICATIONS FOR POLICY:
ECONOMIC DEVELOPMENT

Understanding the effects of changes in the service and manufacturing sectors on income and its distribution can provide directions for policy on economic development. Two questions of critical importance include (1) whether the service sector should be promoted as a means of local economic development, and (2) whether the size or remoteness of a place influences the potential impact of manufacturing and service industries on income multipliers and how income is distributed. The direction and content of policy on economic development should reflect the answers to both these questions.

The relevance of the first question is obvious. There has been debate over the utility of the service sector as a means for promoting economic growth. If service sector growth has a positive effect on social well-being, it can be used as a resource in strategies for economic development. The second question focuses on whether different strategies are needed for rural and urban places. Since the impact of the various sectors differs among these places, optimal economic development strategies for a place would emphasize building those sectors with the greatest potential for increasing social well-being.

The service sector appears to have the capacity to act as a resource in strategies for economic development. Resources for economic development available to rural communities in terms of human capital, monetary resources, and physical infrastructure limit the range of potential strategies available to these places (Pulver, 1986a:12). Strategies that focus on improving the efficiency and attractiveness of downtown businesses, while requiring less of a financial commitment, include advertising, educational programs for local businesspeople on purchasing and marketing techniques, and programs focusing on the retention and expansion of existing businesses in the community (Phillips, 1986:512; Pulver, 1986b:505).

For instance, programs promoting downtown shopping districts encourage the development of firms in the service sector such as retail establishments and restaurants. These firms help sustain the local economy by providing employment, albeit lower-wage employment, and inducing local multipliers by keeping community dollars within the local economy (Pulver, 1986b:505).

Improving the availability of services in the community can also enhance the efficiency of existing firms. The local economy is better able to develop a diversified base by promoting the retention and expansion of existing firms, for instance, in manufacturing. This, at the same time, will help make the local economy more stable over the business cycle (Smith, S.M., unpublished paper).

The service sector, particularly high-wage services, is characterized by jobs requiring higher levels of education and skill (Shelp, 1985:128). Educational programs that enhance the skills of the community's labor force would provide human capital for attracting new service sector employers (Pulver, 1986a:12; Shelp, 1985:128). Incorporating these programs into the curriculum of vocational programs in local high schools for day and night classes is a cost-efficient approach for accomplishing this aim.

However, inducements may be needed for high-wage firms to locate in more remote areas. For instance, the use of federal government subsidies to help attract producer and distributive services, such as wholesale trade, to nonmetropolitan communities could help reduce inequities.

Regardless, development efforts that are likely to produce change will capitalize on the fact that low-wage service industries are growing across the spectrum of places. This growth can be used to promote the development of other industries in the community.

Larger places, on the other hand, are more likely to have the financial resources to actively promote a diversified industrial mix. Strategies that promote the development of an array of service and manufacturing industries are more likely to enhance the community's well-being than efforts focusing solely on manufacturing or the service sector.

New employers in manufacturing and services can be attracted by developing facilities which provide, for example, business services. These facilities have the potential to attract new firms as well as benefit existing ones in the community by improving their efficiency. In fact, the greatest benefit of such centers to the community may occur through the expansion of current businesses, since the largest source of employment growth in both rural and urban areas is the expansion of existing firms (Pulver, 1986a:13; 1986b:503). Further, establishing these service centers would simultaneously create jobs in the high-wage service sector.

However, larger places, which have undergone an economic decline, are probably unable to invest the monetary resources in developing facilities to attract new employers into the community. These places may need to employ strategies similar to those suggested above for smaller and more remote places. These strategies require smaller investments of monetary resources on the part of the community. Once employment levels stabilize and returns to the community are realized, larger monetary investments in strategies for developing a diversified economy could be attempted.

The findings also suggest that centrally located places (defined as being near an interstate highway) are lagging behind in development. At least in this analysis, being centrally located is associated with economic decline. Advantages formerly associated with this location appear to have decreased as manufacturing jobs have left the community. Developing alternative sources of employment, particularly in services, would enhance the attractiveness of these places. With advances in telecommunications, potential employers are better able to locate in communities with a more productive economic climate, even though the location is less central.

Another group of communities also of concern are those experiencing increases in income inequality while undergoing growth in aggregate income levels. In over 40 percent of the communities, economic development was accompanied by an increase in the concentration of income (as measured by an increase in median family income and the variance of the logarithms).

Preliminary evidence suggests that these places are moderately populated. Their industrial structure appears to be characterized by a greater dependency on manufacturing as a source of employment, particularly in low-wage manufacturing. Furthermore, these communities have a lower percentage of women in the work force, thereby indicating that alternative sources of employment, such as various service industries, are not well developed.

A better understanding of the dynamics of industrial conditions and change in these places will be needed in order to formulate economic development policies that do not result in a simultaneous increase of community income and inequality. Based on preliminary evidence, two factors that appear to be associated with simultaneous increases in income and inequality are dependency on a declining economic sector for employment, such as manufacturing, and the presence of barriers to entering the labor force, as indicated by fewer women being in the labor force.

It is important to note, however, that the results indicate that the income potential of many service sector jobs does not appear to match that of jobs in high-wage manufacturing. Places with larger numbers of women in the work force experienced declines in aggregate income during the 1970s.[2] The income distribution in these places appears to have shifted to the lower end, as the number of families in the lower half of the distribution increased relative to the upper half. A positive note is that these distributional changes are associated with decreasing levels of income inequality within the community, due to the increasing homogeneity in the levels of income among families.

IMPLICATIONS FOR POLICY: INCOME MAINTENANCE, HEALTH INSURANCE, AND EDUCATION

The research presented in this book has emphasized the impact of employment growth in the service sector on income. However, the types of benefit packages offered with these jobs also affect well-being. A substantial proportion of jobs in the service sector are part-time, offering few, if any, (employer-provided) health or pension benefits.[3] Part-time workers often are not covered under worker protection programs, such as unemployment insurance (U.S. GAO, 1991). Wage rates for part-time workers are generally low (Appelbaum and Albin, 1990; Christopherson, 1990; U.S. GAO, 1991), which means these workers are less able to purchase health insurance privately, or have savings set aside for unemployment or retirement.

As a consequence of these trends, the immediate and long-term well-being of workers employed in a nontraditional capacity, such as part-time work, will be restricted due to the lack of health insurance, unemployment insurance, and minimal provisions for retirement income.[4] In 1988 about 25 percent of U.S. workers were employed in part-time, temporary, or contract jobs, with this proportion expected to increase through the 1990s (U.S. GAO, 1991).

Moreover, 80 percent of the increase in part-time employment between 1969 and 1987 was due to an increased number of involuntary part-time workers, meaning employees working part-time and desiring although unable to find full-time work. The percentage of involuntary part-time workers without health insurance continued to increase through the 1980s, with over one-third of all involuntary part-time workers having no health insurance in 1987 (U.S. GAO, 1991:22).

Public and private programs for providing health insurance, retirement benefits, and other forms of worker protection (for example, unemployment insurance) have been designed for the traditional full-time worker (U.S. GAO, 1991:10). An increasing proportion of the work force in contingent employment will require that policies regarding the provision of health insurance and income maintenance programs, such as unemployment insurance and retirement provisions, be redesigned to accommodate these workers. Otherwise, the proportion of workers without basic protection will increase. The logical result is an increasing proportion of workers relying on public welfare systems, such as Medicaid and SSI, in order to meet their income maintenance and health care needs.

The importance of education for achieving earnings and occupational advancement is likely to increase in the future, as employment growth continues in the service sector. Policies that promote the increased access of women, minorities, and those from disadvantaged areas to educational institutions will be needed to help combat the emergence of an underclass.

For instance, current employment trends indicate that the rural population will lag further behind the urban population in terms of the potential for earnings and occupational achievement. Without provisions for training in higher-level skills, employment growth in rural areas is likely to concentrate in the low-wage service sector, such as retail trade. The result would be increased underemployment within the rural labor force, due to the prevalence of part-time and low-wage jobs (derived from Findeis, 1991:23). This implies that an increasing proportion of the rural population may be without health insurance, pension benefits, and unemployment insurance.

Hence, strategies will need to promote educational programs in conjunction with other programs aimed at the development of producer and distributive services in rural communities. However, given limited resources in nonmetropolitan areas, a judicious use of resources will require communities to assess their potential for attracting higher-paying sectors, and then concentrate on recruiting just one or two (Smith, S.M., unpub. paper).

This strategy of providing appropriate job skills to the available work force, while simultaneously striving to attract higher-paying producer and distributive service firms, is also appropriate for sections of the urban community. For instance, the shortage of "good" jobs in the inner city contributes to the persistence of poverty and underemployment. However, job skills training for lower-level work in the producer and distributive services (for example, keypunching) still needs to be available.

As increasing numbers of jobs are found in the service sector, training and education will become a stronger determinant of social well-being. The absence of any sort of skills training will isolate those trapped in low-skill, low-wage jobs with no benefits or prospects for advancement from persons able to compete for positions with some advancement potential or benefits. Within the service sector, these better jobs tend to be found in the producer and distributive services. While there is a wide range of occupations within these industries, even the lower-level ones tend to offer more economic rewards than jobs in consumer services.

NOTES

1. This effect of population size persists even after controlling on cost-of-living differentials between communities.

2. Supplemental research indicates that the negative impact of higher proportions of females in the labor force is most apparent in centrally located places, but weakest in more remotely located ones (Kassab, 1990a). These findings reflect the tendency for women to be in lower paying jobs, and the lower paying consumer service sector to have a more positive impact on community income in rural areas.

3. For example in 1988, 36 percent of the workers in service-producing industries were part-time while only 19 percent of all workers fell in this category (U.S. GAO, 1991:4). Part-time workers in the service sector are concentrated in retail trade, and hotels and restaurants, and in lower level occupations (Appelbaum and Albin, 1990; U.S. GAO, 1991).

About 20 percent of all part-time workers do not have any health insurance, with minorities and those who head families even less likely to have health insurance than other part-time workers (U.S. GAO, 1991). Among those working part-time, only 10 percent are included in their employer's pension plan, while 46 percent of full-time workers are covered. In addition, Social Security benefits are low for some nontraditional workers, since they have intermittent work histories, generally in lower-paying positions (U.S. GAO, 1991). Unemployment insurance is also typically not available to part-time workers; declines in the proportion of the unemployed receiving unemployment benefits can partially be attributed to the increasing proportion of part-time workers. In 1988, for instance, only 32 percent of unemployed workers received unemployment insurance, one of the lowest rates since 1955 (U.S. GAO, 1991).

4. If fewer workers receive employer-provided pension benefits, those workers, once they retire, will rely to a greater extent upon Social Security as a source of income. Thus, a larger proportion of elderly in the future may live with economic hardship, having very little money to spend. This means that the viability of relying upon the elderly as a means of economic development may have reduced utility in the future.

Appendix A

Defining and Operationalizing Community: The Mid-Atlantic Sample

In the analysis described in the fourth chapter, communities in the Mid-Atlantic region (New Jersey, New York, and Pennsylvania) constitute the sample.[1] This region was chosen since it experienced a transition from manufacturing to service sector employment.

More precisely, communities constructed in the sample are intended to represent central place areas. A central place area is comprised of an urban area (central place) and its associated hinterland. The central place and surrounding urban fringe exhibit complementarity in economic functions (King, 1984:20). The term "community area," as used by Hawley (1950:245–263), is similar to the concept of central place area. A community area refers to a spatial unit in which residents are functionally interdependent. Boundaries are determined by the routine daily movements in and out of the center of the community.

The central place area is used to define the community, since the objective of this research is to study local societies possessing an ecological unity.[2] While the central place area constitutes an appropriate unit of analysis for this study, no claim is made that it is the only unit which provides an adequate measure of the community area. The objective of the analysis is to explain changes in community-level income and the distribution of income within and across communities. The amount and distribution of income over the expanse of the central place area is a property of this unit. Thus, measuring the dependent variables at the level of the central place area provides conceptually meaningful indicators of community income and its distribution.

Table A.1
Frequency of Central Place Areas in the Mid-Atlantic Region by State

State	Frequency	Percent
New Jersey	98	15%
New York	256	39
Pennsylvania	296	46
Total	650	100%

The communities in the sampling frame were created with an iterative computer algorithm which calculated the population centroid for all census places with a population of 1,000 or more.[3] All census places in each state were rank-ordered by 1970 population size. The procedure started with the most populous places in each state. A five-mile radius was drawn from the centroid of each place. Any minor civil division (MCD) with at least one-half its area falling within that radius was included as part of the urban area surrounding the central place.

By starting with the largest places, some census places were not given the opportunity to be in a central place; instead they were in the urban area of a larger central place (Goode, 1985; 1987). Also, some MCDs were not incorporated into any central place areas since they were below the 1,000 population size criterion for places and were not part of the hinterland for any other central place. The vast majority of the population was included in central places. For instance, in Pennsylvania, over 95 percent of the population resides in one of the central place areas created by the procedure (Fink and Goode, 1975:4).

These procedures, as described by Goode (1985; 1987), resulted in 650 central place areas being delimited in the Mid-Atlantic states. Nearly half (46 percent) of these places are in Pennsylvania (See Table A.1).

Eight communities are excluded from the analysis. New York City and Philadelphia are outliers in population size and, hence, aggregate income. They are excluded from analyses so that regression coefficients are not biased or the R^2s, the coefficients of determination, artificially lowered. Five communities in the Mid-Atlantic are excluded because they had population in a state outside the region.[4] Two of the excluded communities had their center in New York, while the other three communities had their center in Pennsylvania. One community in Pennsylvania was excluded since no Dun and Bradstreet data was available for that place. Excluding these communities resulted in a sample size of 642 communities.

NOTES

1. The analysis in the fifth chapter, however, is a national study; counties rather than communities constitute the unit of analysis.

2. One may question whether central place areas are valid indicators of an ecological whole due to increasing interdependency between places (Hage, 1979:101; Burton, 1963:289). One type of urban settlement pattern thought to become more likely is the dispersed city, defined as functionally interdependent urban places separated by nonurban land (Burton, 1963:289). An increase in the prevalence of dispersed cities would conflict with the use of central place areas as operational definitions of local societies, since the procedures used by Forsht (1972) and Goode (1987) and adopted here to define these units permit only contiguous minor civil divisions (MCDs) to be aggregated into central place areas.

However, the evidence is inconclusive regarding the existence of dispersed cities (Fisher and Mitchelson, 1981:302). Research on American villages suggests that regions of the country not experiencing the population turnaround are retaining a hierarchical settlement structure (Johansen and Fuguitt, 1984:55). Some researchers also found that village growth was not a trend in the northeastern region of the United States (Johansen and Fuguitt, 1984:54). Since the sample for this study is a part of the northeastern U.S., central place areas appear to be a valid indicator of local ecological units.

3. In this study, the center of the community, or the urban area as used in central place theory, is a place, as designated by the U.S. census, regardless of whether the census has defined it as rural or urban. A place is an incorporated political unit or a closely settled population center without corporate limits (unincorporated place). Unincorporated places have a "definite nucleus of residences" (U.S. Bureau of the Census, 1972: App-2).

4. One other community had population in a state neighboring the Mid-Atlantic; it is not excluded since the proportion of the extraregional population in the community is so small as to be essentially zero.

Appendix B

Measuring Employment with Dun and Bradstreet Data Files

The purpose of this appendix is to describe potential sources of error, both systematic and random, in the Dun and Bradstreet data files. Implications of these problems for the reliability and validity of results are given. The procedure used to correct one source of systematic bias in the data base is described.

The data files are maintained by the Dun and Bradstreet Corporation primarily for the purposes of credit ratings and marketing research (Fuller, 1979:1). The data base does not, and is not intended to, represent a census of industries in an area (Birch, 1979:5). For these reasons, it is important to review studies examining the validity and reliability of this data source in order to assess the potential impact of inaccuracies in the data, from the perspective of social science, on the validity of the analysis.

There are several sources of bias and unreliability in the data from Dun and Bradstreet, as there are in any secondary data set. Those problems relevant to the concerns of this study are reviewed here. Inaccuracies in the data tend to be magnified at micro levels of analysis, especially at substate levels (Birch, 1979). Fuller (1979) found in a case study of a Pennsylvanian county that counts of establishments and employment in these establishments were more consistent at the state level than at the county level. The Pennsylvania Industrial Directory was used as a comparison source of data. Furthermore, there was greater consistency at the macro level than at the micro level in figures of percentage change (Fuller, 1979:3).

Birch (1979) in his study of industrial patterns in Connecticut also found greater consistency at macro levels of analysis than at micro levels. Findings of a study comparing Dun and Bradstreet data with those from the Connecticut Department of Commerce indicate that estimates of employment change can be off by as much as a factor of two or three, due to the tendency not to record firm births the year they occur (Birch, 1979:11). Therefore, the figures for any given year tend to be underestimates of the total number of firms and the number of employees. This downward bias in employee counts is of particular relevance to this study, since the objective is to examine change in the number of employees at the community level.

However, Goode (1985) found in an analysis of employment change in small Pennsylvanian communities that the Dun and Bradstreet data files did not affect the accuracy of results. Statistically significant results obtained from Dun and Bradstreet data were not considered different from results using Pennsylvania County Industry Reports, a more traditional source of data.

Another source of inaccuracy is due to some businesses refusing to disaggregate counts of their employees by branch or headquarters location. As a result, employment in some communities, especially those with a heavy reliance on branch establishments for employment, tends to be underestimated, while employment in communities housing the headquarters of these establishments is overestimated. It should be noted that this problem also affects data collected by the Census Bureau (Birch, 1979:12).

An analysis of the severity of this problem indicates that it is not major. Birch (1979:12–13) found that employees in these firms constitute a small proportion of the total in the data files for a given year. Furthermore, the proportion of employees in branch establishments tends to be lower than average among these businesses. In 1976, the percentage of employees in firms refusing to disaggregate was 16 percent, and the percentage of employees in branch establishments was, on average, 5 percent of the total number of employees in the business.

Another source of error in the Dun and Bradstreet files is a result of the incomplete listing of service firms. Because these data files are not intended as a census of the corporate population, some organizations are not covered as extensively as others. In particular, nonprofit organizations are underreported (Birch, 1979:5, 7). Furthermore, one consumer service industry, barber and beauty services, is excluded totally from the listing (Johansen and Fuguitt, 1984:225).

In addition, error is induced by Dun and Bradstreet's effort to expand their coverage since 1969 of all types of firms, especially in the trade and service sectors (Birch, 1979). As a result, finding an increased number of firms could be due to structural change in the industrial mix of a place or simply a result of improved data collection procedures. Ambiguity over the source of change in industrial mix is compounded by the tendency for firm births to be underreported (Birch, 1979).

So, while all firms, and in particular trade and service firms, were more likely to be observed in 1978 than in 1969 due to improved data collection procedures, new firms (representing actual growth in a sector) were less likely to be reported.

Consistent with this, Birch (1979:6) found, in his appraisal of Dun and Bradstreet data for Connecticut between 1969 and 1976, that service and trade firms were still underreported in 1976, despite improved coverage. Thus, while there was a reduction in the number of firms not covered by Dun and Bradstreet, this change was not as large as it possibly could be, at least for trade and service firms.

In order to correct for errors stemming from the expanded coverage, an attempt was made to delineate those firms appearing in the data set as a result of the improved coverage. These "new coverage" firms are headquarters establishments and single establishments which are recorded in the 1978 data set but not the 1969 set, although their start-up date is listed as being prior to 1969. Thus, these firms were probably in existence in 1969 but not included in the counts of Dun and Bradstreet. By excluding new coverage firms from analyses of change over the two periods, bias induced by expanded coverage is lessened.

Another procedure was followed for branch establishments listed in the 1978 data set but not in 1969, since the start-up date is not listed for branches. These branch firms were given the same classification status as their headquarters. If the headquarters establishment was a new coverage, the branch was considered new coverage. This procedure should result in a more conservative estimate of employment growth (Goode, 1989).

Other sources of error include clerical errors and misrepresentation of the business by its reporting agents. Neither problem is trivial or avoidable. Quality control efforts by Dun and Bradstreet and those using the data can help eliminate obvious errors. Also, the level of misrepresentation in the Dun and Bradstreet data has informally been estimated as less than the level occurring in surveys by researchers and government agencies. Dun and Bradstreet can alter the credit rating of a business should it be revealed that incorrect information was purposely provided by the firm (Birch, 1979:15–16).

In summary, inaccuracies in the data decrease the level of reliability of employment counts for micro-level units of analysis, such as used in this study. Furthermore, since some service firms are not covered or not covered extensively by Dun and Bradstreet, a decrease in the reliability of employment estimates is expected to occur for these industries. However, studies reported by Birch (1979) and Goode (1985) indicate that by correcting inherent biases in the data set and not demanding a microscopic analysis of economic change, the data set is a source of reasonably valid data.

Appendix C

Comparing Income Distributions of Families and Unrelated Individuals

The purpose of this appendix is to present results from analyses examining whether the income distributions for families and unrelated individuals are similar.[1] Conceptually it would be desirable to combine families and unrelated individuals in order to obtain results for all household units in the community.[2] However, the following analysis indicates that the income distributions for these two groups differ substantially.

Graphs of the income distribution for unrelated individuals and families in 1979 and 1969 are presented in Figures C.1 and C.2, respectively. If the two groups have the same distribution, the shapes should be similar. As can be seen from Figure C.1, unrelated individuals have a larger proportion of families at the lower end of the income distribution than families. Also, unrelated individuals have proportionately fewer people at the upper income levels, as evidenced by the sharper decline in the curve from the mode for this group. The difference in 1979 median income between the two groups is remarkable. The median income for unrelated individuals is $8,600, and for families, it is $28,200 (in constant 1982 dollars).

From Figure C.2 it is evident that even more dissimilarities existed in 1969 between families and unrelated individuals. The modal point in the distribution for unrelated individuals was at the lowest end of the income distribution, in contrast to the middle portion for families. The discrepancy in median incomes was greater in 1969 than 1979; in 1969, median incomes were $6,600 and $29,000 for unrelated individuals and families, respectively (in constant 1982 dollars). The seg-

Figure C.1
Distribution of Income: Families and Unrelated Individuals, 1979

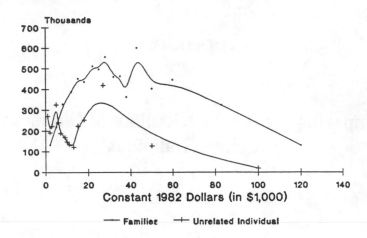

ment of unrelated individuals in the middle of the distribution in 1979 was not evident in 1969.

The decline in the number of middle-income families occurring over the decade can be observed by comparing the distributions for families in Figures C.1 and C.2. The drop in the 1979 distribution at the $35,000-$40,000 range is evidence of bifurcation in the family income distribution. In contrast, a larger proportion of

Figure C.2
Distribution of Income: Families and Unrelated Individuals, 1969

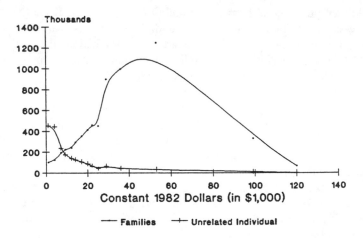

unrelated individuals was found in the middle of the income range in 1979. How-ever, the emergence of this segment probably resulted from increased numbers of elderly, divorced, and younger, single, working adults, such as females postpon-ing marriage to start a career. Income inequality and heterogeneity among unre-lated individuals appear to have increased substantially over the decade.

While income inequality increased for families and unrelated individuals, dif-ferent processes seem to be operating on the distributions for these two groups. The apparent increase in inequality for families is due to the drop in the number of middle-income families, while for unrelated individuals the increase is due to the increased numbers in the middle-income range. These results indicate that the factors influencing the shape of the income distributions for families and unrelated individuals differ considerably, especially in 1969.[3]

Evidence at the community level supports these conclusions. The average in-come for families and unrelated individuals differs significantly in 1969 and 1979, with families possessing a significantly higher income than unrelated individuals (1969: $t = -99.73, df = 641$; 1979: $t = -97.17, df = 641, p < 0.0001$).

In conclusion, these analyses indicate that the income distributions for unre-lated individuals and families differ, both at the community and regional level. It would not be appropriate to combine these two groups, since the resulting distri-bution would not be meaningful—the distributions between the two groups differ too much. As a result, analyses on the structure of income are limited to those generated by families rather than distributions formed by combining families and unrelated individuals.

NOTES

1. Persons not residing in families are classified as unrelated individuals. Inmates of institutions are excluded from counts of either group (U.S. Bureau of the Census, 1970; 1982a).

2. Unrelated individuals are an increasing proportion of the population: between 1969 and 1979, the percentage of unrelated individuals in the Mid-Atlantic region increased from 27 percent to 34 percent.

3. Kassab (1991) conducted a separate analysis for unrelated individuals of the impact of increasing service sector employment on aggregate income. Results, while still prelim-inary, indicate that unrelated individuals residing in an urban area are more likely to benefit from increasing service sector employment than their rural counterparts. These differences are attributed to the demographic profile of unrelated individuals in urban and rural areas, and differences between families and unrelated individuals. It is relevant to note that these results are the opposite of what is reported in the analysis of aggregate income for families, described in the fourth chapter.

Appendix D

Description of General Trends: Changes in the Distribution of Income

General trends in the distribution of income can be observed by examining differences in the percentage of families in each income group over the decade. Figure D.1 graphs the difference (1979–1969) in the mean percentage of families within the lower, middle, upper, and highest income groups over the decade. The lower income group is comprised of the lowest and upper-ower subgroups, while the middle income group is comprised of the lower-middle and upper-middle subgroups. These groups are defined in the third chapter.

When the two lower and middle income subgroups are collapsed into the lower and middle income groups, the decrease in the middle income group appears to be substantially greater than the gains in either the lower or upper income groups. And, the gains at the upper end of the distribution appear to be nearly twice as large as the increase in the lower income group.

However, when changes in the two lower and middle income subgroups are broken apart, it becomes apparent that the gain at the upper end of the lower income group is nearly as great as the gain in the upper income group. Hence, the number of families moving into the lower end of the community income distribution is greater than a preliminary analysis would reveal. The extent to which change occurred in the lower income group is partially suppressed, since the percentage of families at the lowest end of the income distribution decreased[1] and the percentage at the upper end of the lower income group increased.

This analysis supports the contention that the income distribution is becoming more bifurcated. In addition, rather than most of the movement going to the upper

Figure D.1
Change in Mean Percentage of Families in Different Income Groups: 1979–1969

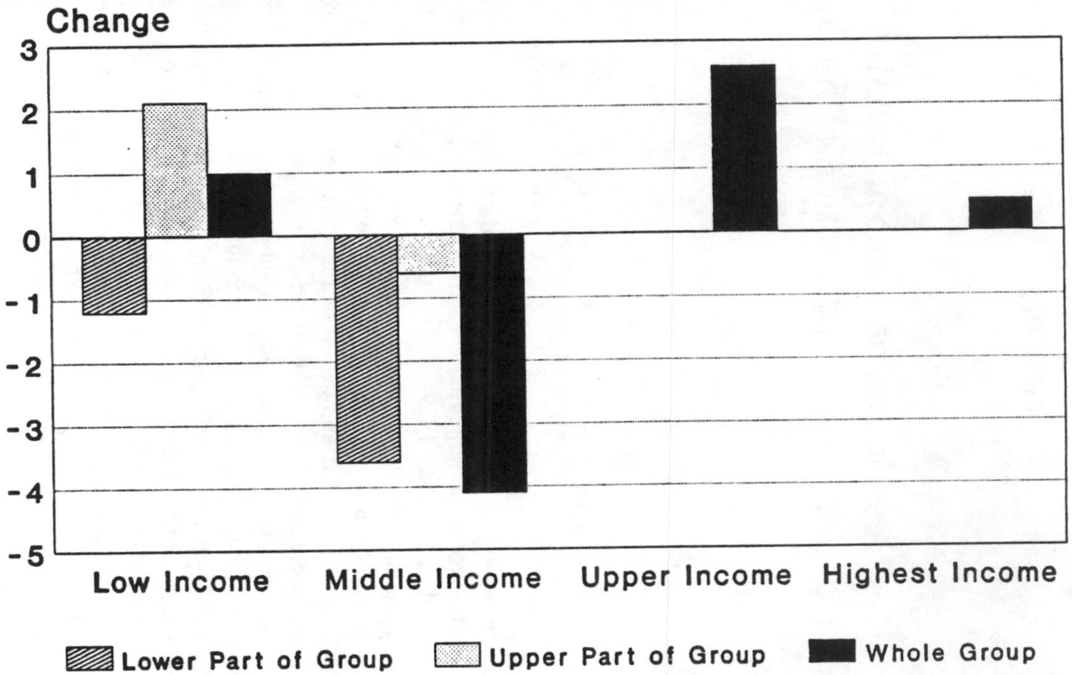

end of the distribution as suggested by some (Horrigan and Haugen, 1988), this analysis indicates that increases in the upper income group only exceed that occurring at the upper end of the lower income group by a small amount.[2]

NOTES

1. Consistent with this finding, the average percentage in poverty for communities in the sample decreased from 7.96 percent to 7.05 percent over the decade.

2. In support of the graphical analysis, the half-share coefficient and variance of the logarithms, two commonly used measures of inequality, indicate an increase in income inequality within communities in the Mid-Atlantic over the decade. The half-share coefficient increased, on average, from 21.5 percent to 23.3 percent; this means that over the 10-year period, the percentage of families experiencing relative financial hardship increased by nearly two percentage points. The variance of the logarithms for family income increased, on average, by 0.036 units.

Hence, these summary indicators and the graphical analysis of the distribution of families across income levels offer consistent evidence that income inequality increased in Mid-Atlantic communities over the 1970 decade.

Appendix E

Results from Cluster Analyses:
Measuring Industrial Mix

Ward's minimum variance method was used to cluster variables measuring characteristics of the community's industrial mix (see, for example, Blashfield, 1976; Milligan, 1981). The variables are listed in Table E.1, along with their means and standard deviations. These variables include percentage employed in low-wage and high-wage branch manufacturing firms, low-wage and high-wage headquarters manufacturing firms, low-wage services, high-wage services, and the percentage of the community population at least 16 years old who were unemployed in 1969.[1] The percentage in the employed population working in various industrial sectors was used in the cluster analysis, rather than the actual number employed in the sector, in order to control on the influence of population size.

The squared Euclidean distance was used to measure the distance between communities in the cluster analysis. The means for the two-cluster through nine-cluster solutions were examined. Results from the four-cluster solution provided interpretable clusters while retaining a sufficient number of cases in each group.

The means for the four-cluster solution are presented in Table E.2. The means for variables defining the major characteristics of each cluster are underlined. The first cluster appears to depict communities with a service-based economy, due to the high percentage of employees in low- and high-wage services. The second cluster appears to consist of communities with diversified local economies; communities in this cluster have higher percentages of employees in services and the various manufacturing sectors. Communities in the third cluster are dependent, on average, on high-wage branch manufacturing, while communities in the fourth

Table E.1
Descriptive Statistics for Variables in Cluster Analysis

Variables	Mean	Standard Deviation
Percentage of Employed Population in:		
High-Wage Branch Manufacturing	32.9	30.9
High-Wage Manufacturing at Headquarters	8.7	15.6
Low-Wage Branch Manufacturing	10.8	19.9
Low-Wage Manufacturing at Headquarters	3.5	9.1
High-Wage Services	13.2	9.8
Low-Wage Services	23.8	15.6
Percentage of Population at Least 16 Years Unemployed	4.1	1.9

cluster appear dependent on low-wage branch manufacturing as a source of employment.

This cluster solution was verified with solutions from two other clustering algorithms. The clustering algorithms used to validate results from Ward's method were the centroid and average linkage between groups clustering methods. The centroid method tends to be robust to outliers, but it may not perform as well in

Table E.2
Means for Variables in Cluster Analysis by Cluster

Variables	Cluster Number (number of cases)			
	1 (233)	2 (219)	3 (143)	4 (47)
Percentage of Employed Population in:				
High-Wage Branch Manufacturing	6.9	35.6	80.6	3.6
High-Wage Manufacturing at Headquarters	5.9	17.0	2.7	1.7
Low-Wage Branch Manufacturing	8.4	6.7	1.6	70.2
Low-Wage Manufacturing at Headquarters	6.1	3.1	0.3	2.1
High-Wage Services	15.5	13.7	9.4	11.5
Low-Wage Services	30.6	20.6	18.7	20.7
Percentage of Population at Least 16 Years Unemployed	4.1	3.8	4.3	4.4

Table E.3
Means for Variables in Centroid and Average Linkage Between Groups Clustering Algorithms

Panel a: Centroid Algorithm

Variables	Cluster Number (number of cases)								
	1	2	3	4	5	6	7	8	9
	(52)	(374)	(137)	(65)	(7)	(4)	(1)	(1)	(1)
Percentage of Employed Population in:									
High-Wage Branch Manufacturing	17.4	21.4	80.7	7.6	---	---	---	---	---
High-Wage Manufacturing at Headquarters	1.6	4.5	0.4	2.3	---	---	---	---	---
Low-Wage Branch Manufacturing	3.5	6.6	1.6	62.0	---	---	---	---	---
Low-Wage Manufacturing at Headquarters	1.6	4.5	0.4	2.3	---	---	---	---	---
High-Wage Services	12.5	14.7	9.6	13.5	---	---	---	---	---
Low-Wage Services	17.9	27.2	16.3	20.3	---	---	---	---	---
Percentage of Population at Least 16 Years									
Unemployed	3.6	4.1	4.3	4.0	---	---	---	---	---

Panel b: Average Linkage Between Groups Algorithm:

Variables	Cluster Number (number of cases)					
	1	2	3	4	5	6
	(65)	(394)	(133)	(47)	(2)	(1)
Percentage of Employed Population in:						
High-Wage Branch Manufacturing	16.4	22.7	81.9	3.3	---	---
High-Wage Manufacturing at Headquarters	1.6	5.1	0.4	2.2	---	---
Low-Wage Branch Manufacturing	3.5	8.1	1.4	70.5	---	---
Low-Wage Manufacturing at Headquarters	1.6	5.1	0.4	2.2	---	---
High-Wage Services	13.9	14.3	9.4	11.7	---	---
Low-Wage Services	20.7	27.2	16.7	20.3	---	---
Percentage of Population at Least 16 Years						
Unemployed	3.6	4.0	4.3	4.4	---	---

other respects as either Ward's method or the solution from average linkage between groups (SAS Institute Inc., 1985:263–264, 267). Whether any of the clusters obtained from Ward's method are dominated by outliers is assessed by comparing the solution from Ward's method with these other two.

The nine-cluster solution using the centroid clustering algorithm produced results that are close to the four-cluster Ward's solution, except for some discrepancies on the first two clusters. The centroid solution has four modal clusters which correspond closely with the third and fourth clusters from Ward's method. The means for the second cluster in the centroid solution are similar to those in Ward's method, although the number of cases is considerably greater. The first cluster, indicating communities with a service-based economy, has far fewer cases than the cluster from Ward's solution, and the dominance of the service sector is not as evident. The other clusters in the centroid solution appear to consist of outliers in the data set; these clusters contain only a few observations. Table E.3a contains the mean and number of cases for each cluster with respect to the clustering variables in the centroid solution.

Results from the six-cluster solution using the average-linkage-between-groups method are presented in Table E.3b. This method produced results that are highly similar to those from the centroid solution. Again, four of the six clusters correspond with the four clusters from Ward's method. The same pattern of similarities and differences appears, as was evidenced by the centroid solution. The other two clusters in the average-linkage method consist of outliers.

In summary, the four-cluster solution using Ward's method produced interpretable clusters. These clusters were validated by two other methods, leading to the conclusion that they consist of natural groupings of communities.

NOTE

1. The percentage employed in single establishments in the manufacturing sector are excluded from the analysis in order to avoid linear dependencies in the data. A single establishment is "a business in which all operations are performed out of one physical location" (Dun's Marketing Services).

Data on percentage unemployed in a community is from the U.S. Census of Population, 1970. The other variables in the cluster analysis are from the Dun and Bradstreet data files.

Appendix F

Supplemental Analysis Using Measures of Income Inequality

This analysis was conducted in order to provide a simplified description of the impact of changes in the employment structure on the income distribution with respect to changes in the level of income inequality. Two indicators used to measure income inequality are the half-share coefficient and the variance of the logarithms. These measures combine the data in different ways to measure inequality, thereby producing different pictures of income inequality in the community. Both are sensitive to changes at the lower end of the income distribution (Bloomquist and Summers, 1982:330; Allison, 1978:868), so results for the two measures should support the other. Change in income inequality over the decade is measured by taking the difference between the 1969 and 1979 indicators (1979–1969).

The half-share coefficient is the proportion of the population receiving less than half of the median income (Atkinson, 1987:760–61; Bloomquist and Summers, 1982:330). This type of indicator is intended to define a point on the income distribution which delimits a group of people considered less "fortunate" than others in the community (Atkinson, 1987:761).[1]

The variance of the logarithms also assigns more weight to transfers at the lower tail of the distribution (Allison, 1978:869). From Atkinson (1970:256), it is defined as

$$V = \left(\frac{\log\left(\frac{y}{u}\right)}{\left(\frac{y}{u}\right)} \right)^2$$

where u is the mean of the distribution. In order to correct for skewness in most income distributions, the natural logarithm is taken. The variance of the logarithms, meaning the variance of the logged income values, measures the concentration of income in the distribution (Aitchison and Brown, 1969:108–20). One advantage of the variance of the logarithms is the statistical properties of the lognormal distribution. Several popular measures of income inequality are functions of the variance of the logarithms; these measures are the Gini coefficient, Theil's measure, and the coefficient of variation (Allison, 1978: 874–75).

REGRESSION ANALYSES

Regression estimates for the half-share coefficient and variance of the logarithms are reported in Table F.1.[2] The estimates for effects of the industry variables are, for the most part, not statistically significant. An exception, however, is that high-wage manufacturing is related to change in the level of inequality for both inequality indicators.

In the model for the half-share coefficient, the only statistically significant industry variable is the number of employees in high-wage manufacturing in 1970 (refer to Table F.1). The negative sign for this effect indicates that communities with higher levels of dependency on the sector tend to experience a decrease in the proportion of families making less than half the median income in the community. That is, income inequality, as measured by the half-share coefficient, decreased over the decade in communities with higher initial levels of employment in high-wage manufacturing.

One explanation for this effect is as follows. The positive correlation between population size and number employed in high-wage manufacturing ($r = 0.85$, $p < 0.0001$) indicates that communities with higher levels of dependency on the sector are bigger places. Larger communities would be more likely to have the infrastructure of the social welfare system to help maintain or supplement incomes if large numbers of workers became unemployed or were laid off. This explanation is supported by the small effect of high-wage manufacturing on aggregate income levels, as reported in the fourth chapter.

Results from the regression on the variance of the logarithms indicates that communities dependent on high-wage branch manufacturing experienced increased income inequality (refer to Table F.1). Results from the fourth chapter indicate that decreasing employment in high-wage manufacturing leads to increasing income inequality as a result of the number of families at the lower end of the distribution increasing while a decrease occurred in the upper half. These results exemplify the negative impact of dependency on a declining economic sector, such as high-wage manufacturing, on the distribution of income in the community. Declines in high-wage manufacturing were more likely to occur in places with a dependency on that sector.[3]

The lack of significant relationships between the industrial change variables and the level of income inequality is somewhat surprising. Analyses of change in

Table F.1
Robust Regression Analyses for the Half-Share Coefficient and Variance of the Logarithms

Variables	Half-Share Coefficient		Var. of Logarithms	
		asymptotic		asymptotic
	Estimate	z-value	Estimate	z-value
Intercept	18.55	3.5	0.35244	15.7
1969 Level of Dependent Variable	-0.65418	-4.2	-0.53631	-17.4
Population Size (1970)	0.00001	0.8	1.25E-7	1.3
Quadratic Effect: Population Size (1970)	---	---	-2.54E-13	-2.1
Change in Population Size (1980 - 1970)	-0.00002	-0.3	1.20E-7	0.4
# Employees in				
High-Wage Manufacturing (1970)	-0.00031	-2.1	-4.62E-7	-0.7
High-Wage Services (1970)	0.00011	0.6	1.18E-6	1.2
Low-Wage Manufacturing (1970)	-0.00024	-0.7	1.51E-6	0.9
Low-Wage Services (1970)	0.00014	0.3	2.52E-6	1.2
Change in # Employees:				
High-Wage Manufacturing (1978 - 1970)	-0.00023	-1.1	-1.27E-7	-0.1
High-Wage Services (1978 - 1970)	-5.97E-6	-0.0	-4.46E-7	-0.5
Low-Wage Manufacturing (1978 - 1970)	-0.00054	-0.9	-1.11E-6	-0.4
Low-Wage Services (1978 - 1970)	-0.00034	-1.2	3.20E-7	0.3
Distance from Interstate Highway	0.00626	0.3	0.00032	2.9
High-Wage Manufacturing Dummy	-1.02631	-1.1	0.01100	2.4
Percentage of Employees in				
HQ Firms in LMA (1970)	-0.11823	-1.9	-0.00130	-4.6
Median Value of Home	-0.00006	-2.3	-2.76E-7	-1.9
Percentage in 1970:				
Females in Work Force	-0.04402	-0.4	-0.00232	-4.3
Minority Population	-0.02540	-0.3	0.00379	8.9
Elderly Population	0.15795	1.0	0.00254	3.6
Percentage Change between 1970 and 1980:				
Females in Work Force	-0.02262	-1.2	-0.00036	-4.2
Minority Population	0.00036	0.3	0.00001	2.2
Elderly Population	0.02200	1.1	0.00008	0.9
Percentage (Number) of Cases Downweighted:	5.0 (32)		5.6 (36)	

the number of families in each income group, reported in the fourth chapter, offered rich results in terms of the number and types of statistically significant effects. The lack of significant findings for the income inequality measures could indicate that these variables are relatively insensitive to changes in the community income distribution when grouped income data are used.

Another problem with the summary measures of inequality is that the effects of industrial sectors vary by income group. For example, the effect of employment growth in low-wage services differs among the lowest, upper-lower, and lower-middle income groups. However, both the half-share coefficient and variance of the logarithms is sensitive to changes in this part of the income distribution (Allison, 1978:868; Bloomquist and Summers, 1982:330). If the effects for these income groups are averaged, the effect of low-wage services would be reduced, if not nullified. This draws into question the typically strong reliance on summary indicators of inequality to measure change or differences among income distributions.

NOTES

1. The centroid of the distribution provides the basis for calculating the half-share coefficient. Since income distributions typically are skewed, the median was chosen to measure the centroid rather than the mean. In support of this decision, Atkinson (1987) used the median as the base for the half-share coefficient.

2. The standard errors for the regression coefficients were obtained through the bootstrapping procedures described in Appendix G. Asymptotic z-values were calculated using the bootstrapped standard errors.

3. Controlling on all population size and change variables in the original model, the partial correlation coefficient for this relationship is -0.145 ($p < 0.001$).

Appendix G

Technical Discussion of
Robust Statistical Procedures

As discussed in the third chapter, the presence of outliers, particularly in the variables measuring employment and change in employment in the different industrial sectors, indicates the need for robust statistical procedures. The first section provides a brief discussion of the robust regression procedure used in this study, that being bounded influence regression. The second section briefly describes and justifies the bootstrapping procedure used to estimate standard errors for the bounded influence regression coefficients.

BOUNDED INFLUENCE REGRESSION

The purpose of using robust regression analysis is to avoid bias in the regression coefficients caused by outliers in the data set. Ordinary least squares (OLS) allow outliers to exert a disproportionate amount of influence on regression results. This occurs because the procedure is designed to minimize the sum of squared residuals (Myers, 1986:201), so the regression line is forced towards outlying observations in order to drive the sum of squared residuals down. Kassab (1990c) demonstrates that the bias in regression coefficients due to the presence of outliers can result in misleading conclusions, and that substantive implications for strategies of economic development can be affected.

There are a variety of procedures for conducting a robust regression. The kind of robust regression considered here is bounded influence regression. Bounded influence regression incorporates both the size of the standardized residual and the leverage of a particular case into the criteria for determining outliers. Leverage indicates the extent to which regression results are influenced by that case (Belsley et al., 1980:17; Myers, 1986:210). Ideally, each case has equal leverage on the regression line (Belsley et al., 1980:17).

Weighted least squares (WLS) are used to produce bounded influence estimates of the regression coefficients in the analysis. The weight in the WLS analysis is based on a function of DFFITS; the value of DFFITS for an observation measures the standardized change in the fit of the OLS regression when that case is deleted from the analysis (Belsley et al., 1980:15; Sheather and Hettmansperger 1987:5–6).[1]

If an observation has a large residual relative to the other observations, a high leverage, or both the residual and leverage are moderate but act in combination, DFFITS will tend to be large (Belsley et al. 1980:265; Myers 1986:150, 284). The algorithm used here downweights an observation to the extent that DFFITS exceeds the tuning constant, the criterion for defining an outlier. If DFFITS for a given observation is less than the tuning constant, the case is not downweighted.

The particular value for the tuning constant used in this analysis was $2[(p + 1)/n]^{1/2}$, where p is the number of variables in the regression model and n is the sample size. This formula for the tuning constant is a size-adjusted cut-off since it corrects for the influence sample size has on the proportion of cases identified as outliers (Belsley et al. 1980:28–29; Kassab, 1990c:374). Using a size-adjusted cutoff rather than an absolute cutoff for demarcating outliers, which does not account for the influence of sample size, allows one to determine which observations are influential in relation to other cases when the sample size is large. It also adjusts for p, the number of variables; this is desirable since DFFITS increases as p increases (Belsley et al. 1980:28–29).

Differences in coefficients between bounded influence and OLS regressions are due to the decreased weight of the outliers in the analysis. When differences between the OLS and bounded influence regression are minor, the OLS results are preferred due to the desirable qualities of regression estimates produced from OLS, these being that OLS estimates have minimum variance among linear unbiased estimators (Myers, 1986).

The SAS program used to produce the robust estimates is listed at the top of the next page.

```
DATA ;
   INPUT Y X1 X2 ... XP ;
CARDS ;
  (data)
;
PROC REG ;
    MODEL Y = X1 X2 ... XP/INFLUENCE ;
        OUTPUT OUT = ROBUST DFFITS = DFITS ;
DATA R ;
  SET ROBUST ;
ADF = ABS(DFITS) ;
C = 2*(SQRT((p + 1)/n)) ;              * Specify p & n ;
WT = MIN(1,(C/ADF)) ;
PROC REG DATA = R ;
    MODEL Y = X1 X2 ... XP ;
WEIGHT WT ;
```

BOOTSTRAPPING STANDARD ERRORS FOR REGRESSION COEFFICIENTS

SAS or any other prepackaged statistical software program provides standard errors and t-values for the bounded influence (weighted) regression that are not correct. The weights used in the bounded influence regression are based on a random variable, the residuals, rather than a fixed quantity, which is assumed in standard WLS procedures (Carroll et al., 1988:1045; Myers, 1986:171–72; Sheather and Hettmansperger, 1987). As a result, t-values reported on the computer output tend to be too large, since the standard errors for the regression coefficients are generally underestimated (Carroll et al., 1988:1045).

One way to correct for this problem is to obtain standard errors for regression coefficients by bootstrapping. The bootstrapping procedure used here produces a nonparametric estimate of the standard error for the regression coefficients by repeatedly sampling, with replacement, the residuals from the robust regression.[2] Regression coefficients for the model are estimated for each sample. The variance for each regression coefficient is calculated from the coefficients obtained from the bootstrapped samples (Efron and Gong, 1983; Stine, 1989).

Another procedure used to produce bootstrapped estimates draws random samples, with replacement, from the observations (rather than the residuals). This procedure is considered appropriate when survey data are used for the independent variables, as is the case in the analyses reported here (Dietz et al.). However, asymptotically there is no difference between the two procedures (Efron and Gong, 1983:43), so the two bootstrapping procedures are expected to yield quite similar results for this research.

NOTES

1. The acronym is comprised of three parts. *FIT* in DFFITS indicates the fitted or predicted value of the dependent variable for a particular case. *DF* refers to the difference in fitted values with a particular case included in the regression analysis and with it excluded. The *S* means the difference in fitted values is standardized (Myers, 1986:284).

2. The bootstrapping algorithm was repeated 990 to 1,056 times for the various dependent variables.

Appendix H

Supplementary Tables

Table H.1 records the median value of dependent and independent variables at various distances from an interstate highway using data from the Mid-Atlantic region. Table H.2 depicts the relationship between population size and percentage change in low-wage and high-wage service sectors for the Mid-Atlantic region. Changes in low-wage services appear to be more evenly distributed across different size classes than changes in the high-wage service sector.[1] This observation is based on the tendency for the adjusted standardized residuals in Table H.2a to be low while the many of the residuals in Table H.2b are considerably higher.[2] The smallest places (less than 20,000) experienced more declines and less fast growth in high-wage services than expected by chance. In contrast, moderately sized places (20,000–100,000) experienced fewer declines than expected in the sector but a greater proportion of fast growth. The largest places did not depart radically from expected values.

Table H.3 provides descriptive statistics for variables used in the national study of nonmetropolitan and metropolitan counties, described in the fifth chapter.

NOTES

1. These data are from Kassab (1989).

2. Adjusted standardized residuals are normalized to have a variance of one. Values exceeding +2 or −2 indicate that the observed count deviates from the expected value under the model of independence (Browne, 1981:158).

Table H.1
Average Characteristics of Communities by Distance from Interstate Highway

Variable	0 (95)	1-3 (81)	4-10 (160)	11-20 (146)	21-35 (90)	35+ (70)
			Distance from Highway in Miles (n)			
Change in aggregate family income (1979-1969) (in $1,000)	$ 6,522	17,398	26,559	13,414	5,379	4,339
Change in median family income (1979-1969)	- $ 322	3,177	3,059	3,036	- 715	- 95
Change in one-half share coefficient (1979-1969)	0.20	2.84	2.31	2.46	0.73	0.69
Change in variance of logarithms (1979-1969)	0.40	0.04	0.04	0.04	0.02	0.04
Percentage of communities whose income distribution is:						
Bifurcating	46%	47	41	44	39	40
Increasing	23%	35	42	32	29	33
Decreasing	24%	14	12	14	19	19
Other form of change	6%	5	4	10	13	9
Change in rank in income hierarchy (1979-1969)	- 3	3	4	- 1	- 12	- 2
Number of Employees in 1970:						
High-wage manufacturing	2,676	507	906	404	472	128
High-wage services	448	143	270	146	124	70
Low-wage manufacturing	361	151	206	102	155	83
Low-wage services	830	311	425	213	228	165
Change in number of employees in (1978-1970)						
High-wage manufacturing	- 147	6	- 19	- 2	2	- 4
High-wage services	845	159	404	90	114	48
Low-wage manufacturing	- 36	0	- 6	- 4	- 10	- 2
Low-wage services	225	114	134	71	84	37
Percentage of communities whose economy is:						
Service-based	37%	37	32	40	41	30
Dependent on high-wage branch manufacturing	20%	18	23	23	19	30
Dependent on low-wage branch manufacturing	1%	1	6	9	10	19
Diversified	42%	43	38	27	30	21
Population size (1970)	26,505	12,230	16,628	8,926	9,038	5,954
Change in population (1980-1970)	292	1,040	980	455	486	306
Median value of home (1970)	$ 42,578	38,876	40,562	35,646	33,598	30,146
Percentage of employees in HQ firms (1970)	17%	16	17	17	16	13
Distance from interstate highway (miles)	0	1	6	15	26	52
Percentage in 1970:						
Females in labor force	37%	35	36	36	36	37
Minorities in population	2%	1	1	1	1	0.5
Elderly in population	11%	10	10	10	11	12
Percentage change (1980-1970):						
Females in labor force	29%	44	38	34	30	30
Minorities in population	51%	84	65	46	50	78
Elderly in population	21%	25	26	22	22	22

a. The median is used due to the presence of outliers in some variables.

Table H.2

Change in Low (a) and High (b) Wage Service Sectors by 1970 Population Size

a

	<20,000	20,000-100,000	>100,000
-100% to 10%	22.1% *1.0*	16.6% *-1.6*	25.4% *0.9*
10% to 50%	32.1% *-3.3*	44.2% *2.3*	49.2% *2.1*
50% to 100%	25.5% *1.2*	22.1% *-0.7*	18.6% *-1.0*
>100%	20.2% *1.8*	17.2% *-0.4*	6.8% *-2.4*

The Cell Percentage is Based on the Column Total

The Figures in Italics are Adjusted Standardized Residuals

b

	<20,000	20,000-100,000	>100,000
-100% to 10%	23.6% *5.3*	6.7% *-4.3*	6.8% *-2.3*
10% to 100%	35.5% *-0.5*	31.9% *-1.3*	52.5% *2.8*
100% to 250%	18.3% *-5.5*	41.1% *5.4*	30.5% *1.0*
>250%	22.6% *1.5*	20.2% *-0.2*	10.2% *-2.1*

The Cell Percentage is Based on the Column Total

The Figures in Italics are Adjusted Standardized Residuals

Table H.3

Descriptive Statistics for Variables in Nonmetropolitan and Metropolitan County Models

Variables	Mean	Median	Std. Dev.	Minimum Value	Maximum Value	Sample Size
NONMETROPOLITAN COUNTIES:						
Change in Wage and Salary Disbursements (1988-1979)						
(in $100,000)	31.74	-7.92	4.13	-2,977	5,220	2,358
Population Size (1979)						
(in 1,000)	221.95	156	207.52	0	1,617	2,358
Change in Population Size (1988-1979)						
(in 1,000)	11.99	2	39.85	-161	566	2,358
Number of Employees (1978)						
Manufacturing	1,816	777	2,636	2	20,168	2,309
High-Wage Services	1,465	849	1,698	10	12,949	2,345
Low-Wage Services	1,373	784	1,591	10	15,294	2,344
Change in Number of Employees (1987-1978)						
Manufacturing	-107	-12	775	-6,688	6,738	2,294
High-Wage Services	420	168	850	-3,885	13,420	2,345
Low-Wage Services	261	64	709	-1,606	12,559	2,344
Disaggregation of Service Industries: Number of Employees (1978):						
Transportation, Communications, and Public						
Utilities (TCPU)	281	162	355	2	4,691	2,322
Wholesale Trade	297	178	343	5	2,850	2,317
Finance, Insurance, and Real						
Estate (FIRE)	244	140	285	10	4,537	2,328
Business and Professional						
Services	112	42	223	2	4,208	2,274
Medical and Health Services	336	175	452	3	4,001	2,274
Social Services	157	66	301	3	8,114	2,107
Retail Trade	1,111	645	1,265	10	12,512	2,344
Personal Services	265	128	410	4	7,617	2,318
Disaggregation of Service Industries: Change in # Employees (1987-1978):						
Transportation, Communications, and Public Utilities						
(TCPU)	34	8	226	-2,407	3,477	2,314
Wholesale Trade	12	0	147	-839	1,680	2,300
Finance, Insurance, and Real						
Estate (FIRE)	51	16	167	-1,669	2,838	2,321
Business and Professional						
Services	87	21	223	-2,148	3,369	2,259
Medical and Health Services	142	66	252	-459	3,057	2,254
Social Services	69	20	310	-970	10,308	2,069
Retail Trade	218	58	568	-950	9,783	2,344
Personal Services	43	4	205	-662	3,524	2,310

Table H.3 continued

Variables	Mean	Median	Std. Dev.	Minimum Value	Maximum Value	Sample Size
METROPOLITAN COUNTIES:						
Change in Wage and Salary Disbursements (1988-1979):						
(in $100,000)	4,319.26	723.69	144.69	-44,032	208,140	721
Population Size (1979)						
(in 1,000)	2,357.29	1,112	4,506.61	43	74,010	721
Change in Population Size (1988-1979)						
(in 1,000)	250.50	82	715.49	-2,304	11,868	721
Number of Employees (1978)						
Manufacturing	22,530	7,897	54,311	7	887,538	719
High-Wage Services	30,536	8,758	81,949	50	1,133,658	719
Low-Wage Services	19,703	8,263	41,120	59	681,859	719
Change in Number of Employees (1987-1978)						
Manufacturing	-1,873	-107	13,546	-222,957	71,502	719
High-Wage Services	12,873	3,529	29,595	-20,735	448,075	719
Low-Wage Services	5,758	2,238	11,296	-3,243	169,910	719
Disaggregation of Service Industries: Number of Employees (1978):						
Transportation, Communications, and						
Public Utilities (TCPU)	5,149	1,504	12,737	10	163,147	719
Wholesale Trade	5,476	1,452	14,490	10	203,511	719
Finance, Insurance, and Real						
Estate (FIRE)	5,847	1,354	20,031	10	378,731	719
Business and Professional						
Services	4,826	836	16,226	10	261,042	719
Medical and Health Services	5,467	1,873	12,018	6	183,477	715
Social Services	2,432	629	6,523	10	78,734	715
Retail Trade	15,505	6,824	30,645	39	480,909	719
Personal Services	4,164	1,422	10,840	16	200,594	719
Disaggregation of Service Industries: Change in # Employees (1987-1978):						
Transportation, Communications, and						
Public Utilities (TCPU)	643	183	3,690	-41,133	46,413	719
Wholesale Trade	1,202	211	4,188	-27,725	62,774	718
Finance, Insurance, and Real						
Estate (FIRE)	2,241	322	7,345	-2,831	140,765	718
Business and Professional						
Services	4,391	907	11,268	-1,830	161,866	719
Medical and Health Services	2,641	1,018	4,782	-441	66,056	715
Social Services	1,237	383	2,913	-2,700	37,098	714
Retail Trade	4,341	1,848	7,803	-3,117	100,319	719
Personal Services	1,399	361	4,119	-1,955	69,103	719

Bibliography

Advisory Commission on Intergovernmental Relations (ACIR). *A commission report. Regional growth: historic perspective.* Washington, DC, 1980.

Aitchison, J., and J. A. C. Brown. *The lognormal distribution.* Cambridge: University Press, 1969.

Aldrich, J. H., and F. D. Nelson. *Linear probability, logit, and probit models.* Beverly Hills, CA: Sage Publications, Inc., 1984.

Allison, P. D. Measures of inequality. *American Sociological Review* 43(Dec.):865–80, 1978.

Appelbaum, E., and P. Albin. Shifts in employment, occupational structure, and educational attainment. In *Skills, wages, and productivity in the service sector*, ed. T. Noyelle. Boulder: Westview Press, 1990.

Appelbaum, R. P. City size and urban life: a preliminary inquiry into some consequences of growth in American cities. *Urban Affairs Quarterly* 12(2):139–70, 1976.

Atkinson, A. B. On the measurement of inequality. *Journal of Economic Theory* 2:224–63, 1970.

Atkinson, A. B. On the measurement of poverty. *Econometrica* 55(4):749–64, 1987.

Barkley, D. L. Plant ownership characteristics and the locational stability of rural Iowa manufacturers. *Land Economics* 54(Feb.):92–99, 1978.

Bell, D. *The coming of post-industrial society.* New York: Basic Books, Inc., 1973.

Belsley, D. A., E. Kuh, and R. E. Welsch. *Regression diagnostics: identifying influential data and sources of collinearity.* New York: John Wiley and Sons, 1980.

Bender, L. D. The role of services in rural development policies. *Land Economics* 63(1):62–71, 1987.

Bednarzik, R. A special focus on employment growth in business services and retail trade. In *Skills, wages, and productivity in the service sector*, ed. T. Noyelle. Boulder: Westview Press, 1990.

Beyers, W. B., and M. J. Alvine. Export services in postindustrial society. *Papers of the Regional Science Association* 57:33–45, 1985.

Birch, D. L. Using Dun and Bradstreet data for micro analyses of regional and local economies. M.I.T. Program on Neighborhood and Regional Change, Cambridge, MA, 1979.

Blashfield, R. K. Mixture model tests of cluster analysis: accuracy of four agglomerative hierarchical methods. *Psychological Bulletin* 83(3):377–88, 1976.

Blau, P. M. Implications of growth in services for social structure. *Social Science Quarterly* 61(1):3–22, 1980.

Bloomquist, L. E. Labor market characteristics and the occupational concentration of different sociodemographic groups. *Rural Sociology* 55(2):199–213, 1990.

Bloomquist, L. E., and G. F. Summers. Organization of production and community income distributions. *American Sociological Review* 47(June):325–38, 1982.

Bluestone, B., and B. Harrison. The new jobs are paying less. *New York Times* February 1:F3, 1987.

Bradley, T., and P. Lowe. *Locality and rurality: economy and society in rural regions*. Regency House: Norwich, England, 1984.

Browne, L. E. Taking in each other's laundry—the service economy. *New England Economic Review* July/August:20–31, 1986.

Browne, M. B. *BMDP statistical software*. University of California Press: Berkeley, 1981.

Brown, D. L., and K. L. Deavers. Rural change and rural economic policy agenda for the 1980s. In *Rural economic development in the 1980s: preparing for the future*. Washington, DC: U.S. Department of Agriculture, Economic Research Service, Staff Report No. AGES870724, 1987.

Brue, S. L. Local employment and payroll impacts of corporate mergers. *Growth and Change* 6(Oct.):8–13, 1975.

Burton, I. A restatement of the dispersed city hypothesis. *Annals of the Association of American Geographers* 53(3):285–89, 1963.

Campbell, D. T., and J. C. Stanley. *Experimental and quasi-experimental designs for research*. Boston: Houghton Mifflin Company, 1963.

Carroll, R. J., C. F. J. Wu, and D. Ruppert. The effect of estimating weights in weighted least squares. *Journal of the American Statistical Association* 83(404):1045–54, 1988.

Christaller, W. (trans. by C. W. Baskin). *Central places in southern Germany*. Englewood Cliffs: Prentice Hall, 1966.

Christopherson, S. Emerging patterns of work. In *Skills, wages, and productivity in the service sector*, ed. T. Noyelle. Boulder: Westview Press, 1990.

Collver, A., and M. Semyonov. Suburban change and persistence. *American Sociological Review* 44(June):480–86, 1979.

Couto, R. A. Toward a human service economy. In *Communities in economic crisis: Appalachia and the South*, ed. J. Gaventa, B. E. Smith, and A. Willingham. Philadelphia: Temple University Press, 1990.

Danziger, S. Determinants of the level and distribution of family income in metropolitan areas, 1969. *Land Economics* 52(4):467–78, 1976.

Dietz, T., L. Kalof, and R. S. Frey. On the utility of robust and resampling strategies. Unpublished paper.

Dun's Marketing Services. Magnetic tape description. The Dun and Bradstreet Corporation, Parsippany, NJ.

Efron, B., and G. Gong. A leisurely look at the bootstrap, the jackknife, and cross-validation. *The American Statistician* 37(1):36–48, 1983.

Farnsworth, C. H. Freer world trade falls victim to its own success. *New York Times* November 27, 1990.

Feketekuty, G. International trade in services. In *United States: service industries handbook*, ed. W. O. Candilis. New York: Praeger, 1988.

Findeis, J. Utilization of rural labor resources. University Park: The Pennsylvania State University, Department of Agricultural Economics and Rural Sociology, Staff Paper No. 201, 1991.

Fink, J. C., and F. M. Goode. Estimated employment loss in Pennsylvania communities resulting from proposed abandonment of potentially excess rail lines. University Park: The Pennsylvania State University, Department of Agricultural Economics and Rural Sociology, AE & RS Bulletin 114, 1975.

Firebaugh, G. and J. P. Gibbs. User's guide to ratio variables. *American Sociological Review* 50(Oct.):713–22, 1985.

Fisher, J. S., and R. L. Mitchelson. Forces of change in the American settlement pattern. *Geographic Review* 71(3):298–310, 1981.

Forsht, G. Measurement of economic activity of the central place areas in Pennsylvania, 1960–1970. Ph.D. diss., The Pennsylvania State University, 1972.

Frey, W. H. Migration and depopulation of the metropolis: regional restructuring or rural renaissance? *American Sociological Review* 52(April):240–57, 1987.

Fuguitt, G. V. The nonmetropolitan population turnaround. *Annual Review of Sociology* 11:259–80, 1985.

Fuller, T. E. On the accuracy of the Dun and Bradstreet DMI files: a case study. Paper presented at the Dun and Bradstreet Dun's Market Identifiers File, Data Users Conference, Advisory Commission in Intergovernmental Relations, Washington, DC, 1979.

Fuller, T. E. *The Northeast: two decades of slow employment growth*. Ithaca, New York: Cornell University, Northeast Center for Regional Development, Publication 31, 1982.

Fuller, T. E. *The Mid-Atlantic region in transition: employment trends, 1974–84*. Washington, DC: U.S. Department of Agriculture, Economic Research Service, Research Report No. 57, 1986.

Fuller, T. E., and W. R. Gillis. Road to Renaissance: Growth Industries for Pennsylvania. University Park, PA: The Pennsylvania State University, Department of Agricultural Economics and Rural Sociology, 1986.

Gillespie, A. E., and A. E. Green. The changing geography of producer services employment in Britain. *Regional Studies* 21(5):397–411, 1987.

Gillis, W. R. Can service-producing industries provide a catalyst for regional economic growth? *Economic Development Quarterly* 1(3):249–56, 1987.

Ginzberg, E. and G. J. Vojta. The service sector of the U.S. economy. *Scientific American* 244(3):48–55, 1981.

Glasmeier, A., and G. Borchard. Research policy and review 31. From branch plants to back offices: prospects for rural services growth. *Environment and Planning A* 21:1565–583, 1989.

Goode, F. M. The use of microdata to measure employment changes in small communities. *Journal of Economic and Social Measurement* 13:187–97, 1985.

Goode, F. Personal communication regarding procedures for delineating communities, The Pennsylvania State University, Department of Agricultural Economics and Rural Sociology, 1987.

Goode, F. Personal communication regarding procedures for manipulating data from Dun and Bradstreet files, The Pennsylvania State University, Department of Agricultural Economics and Rural Sociology, 1989.

Gruenstein, J. M. L., and S. Guerra. Can services sustain a regional economy. *Business Review* July/August:15–27, 1981.

Hage, J. A theory of nonmetropolitan growth. In *Nonmetropolitan industrial growth and community change*, ed. G. F. Summers and A. Selvik. Lexington, MA: Lexington Books, 1979.

Hanushek, E. A., and J. E. Jackson. *Statistical Methods for Social Scientists*. New York: Academic Press, 1977.

Haren, C. C. Rural industrial growth in the 1960s. *American Journal of Agricultural Economics* 52(3):431–37, 1970.

Hawley, A. H. *Human ecology*. New York: The Ronald Press Company, 1950.

Hawley, A. H. *Human ecology: a theoretical essay*. Chicago: The University of Chicago Press, 1986.

Hayghe, H. V. Family members in the work force. *Monthly Labor Review* March, 1990.

Hirschl, T. A., and S. A. McReynolds. Service employment and rural community economic development. *Journal of the Community Development Society* 20(2):15–30, 1989.

Hoppe, R. A. *The role of the elderly's income in rural development*. Agriculture and Rural Economy Division, Economic Research Service. U.S. Department of Agriculture. Rural Development Research Report No. 80, 1991.

Horrigan, M. W., and S. E. Haugen. The declining middle-class thesis: a sensitivity analysis. *Monthly Labor Review* 111(5):3–13, 1988.

Howes, C., and A. R. Markusen. Poverty: a regional political economy perspective. In *Nonmetropolitan America in transition*, ed. A. H. Hawley and S. M. Mazie. Chapel Hill: The University of North Carolina Press, 1981.

Johansen, H. E., and G. V. Fuguitt. *The changing rural village in America*. Cambridge, MA: Ballinger Publishing Company, 1984.

Kassab, C. The impact of change in the service sector of the local economy on the distribution of income. Paper presented at the American Association for the Advancement of Science Annual Meeting, 1989.

Kassab, C. Can the service sector substitute for manufacturing as a source of income? Paper presented at the Penn State Graduate Research Exhibit, 1990a.

Kassab, C. The impact of changing levels of employment in services and manufacturing on income and its distribution in communities of the Mid-Atlantic region. Ph.D. diss., The Pennsylvania State University, 1990b.

Kassab, C. Studying economic change: are robust regression procedures needed? *Rural Sociology* 55(3):357–75, 1990c.

Kassab, C. The differential impact of growth in the service sector on economic well-being of families and unrelated individuals. Paper presented at the annual meeting of the Southern Sociological Society, 1991.

Kessler, R. C., and D. F. Greenberg. *Linear panel analysis*. New York: Academic Press, 1981.

King, L. J. *Central place theory*. Beverly Hills: Sage Publications, 1984.

Kutscher, R. E. Overview and implications of the projections to 2000. *Monthly Labor Review* 110(9):3–9, 1987.

Kutscher, R. E., and V. A. Personick. Deindustrialization and the shift to services. *Monthly Labor Review* 109(6):3–13, 1986.

Landefeld, J. S. and K. H. Young. U.S. trade in services: 1970–1985. *United States: service industries handbook*, ed. W. O. Candilis. New York: Praeger, 1988.

Li, P. S. and B. D. MacLean. Changes in the rural elderly population and their effects on the small town economy: the case of Saskatchewan. *Rural Sociology* 54(2):213–26, 1989.

Lincoln, J. R. The urban distribution of headquarters and branch plants in manufacturing: mechanisms of metropolitan dominance. *Demography* 15(2):213–22, 1978.

Lincoln, J. R and R. Friedland. Metropolitan dominance and income levels in nonmetropolitan cities. *Sociology and Social Research* 61(3):304–19, 1977.

Logan, J. R. Growth, politics, and the stratification of places. *American Journal of Sociology* 84(2):404–16, 1978.

Long, N. E. Labor intensive and capital intensive urban economic development. *Economic Development Quarterly* 1(3):196–202, 1987.

Lorence, J. Growth in service sector employment and MSA gender earnings inequality: 1970–1980. *Social Forces* 69(3):763–83, 1991.

Marquand, J. Four and a half myths about the service sector. *CES Review* 7:32–36, 1979.

Marshall, J. N. *Services and Uneven Development*. Oxford: Oxford University Press, 1988.

McGranahan, D. A. The spatial structure of income distribution in rural regions. *American Sociological Review* 45(April):313–24, 1980.

McGranahan, D. A. Absentee and local ownership of industry in northwestern Wisconsin. *Growth and Change* 13(April):31–35, 1982.

McMahon, P. J., and J. H. Tschetter. The declining middle class: a further analysis. *Monthly Labor Review* 109(9):22–27, 1986.

Menchik, M. D. The service sector. In *Nonmetropolitan America in transition*, ed. A. H. Hawley and S. M. Mazie. Chapel Hill: The University of North Carolina Press, 1981.

Miller, J. P. *Nonmetro job growth and locational change in manufacturing firms*. Washington, DC: U.S. Department of Agriculture, Economic Development Division, Economics, Statistics, and Cooperative Service, Research Report No. 24, 1980.

Miller, J. P., and H. Bluestone. Prospects for service sector employment growth in nonmetro America. In *Rural economic development in the 1980s: preparing for the future*. Washington, DC: U.S. Department of Agriculture, Economic Research Service, Staff Report No. AGES870724, 1987.

Milligan, G. W. A review of Monte Carlo tests of cluster analysis. *Multivariate Behavioral Research* 16(July):379–407, 1981.

Moore, R. Industrial growth and development policies in the British periphery. In *The rural sociology of the advanced societies: critical perspectives*, ed. F. H. Buttel and H. Newby. Montclair, NJ: Allanheld, Osmun and Co. Publishers, Inc., 1980.

Moriarty, B. M. Hierarchies of cities and the spatial filtering of industrial development. *Papers of the Regional Science Association* 53:59–82, 1983.

Myers, R. H. *Classical and modern regression with applications*. Boston: Duxbury Press, 1986.

Nelson, J. I., and J. Lorence. Employment in service activities and inequality in metropolitan areas. *Urban Affairs Quarterly* 21(1):106–25, 1985.

Nelson, J. I., and J. Lorence. Metropolitan earnings inequality and service sector employment. *Social Forces* 67(2):492–511, 1988.

Neter, J., W. Wasserman, and M. H. Kutner. *Applied linear statistical models*. 2nd ed. Homewood, IL: Irwin, 1985.

Noyelle, T. J. Advanced services in the system of cities. In *Local economies in transition: policy realities and development potentials*, ed. E. M. Bergman. Durham: Duke University Press, 1986a.

Noyelle, T. Economic transformation. In *The Annals*, ed. R. D. Lambert and A. W. Heston, vol. 488. Newbury Park, CA: Sage, 1986b.

Noyelle, T. Overview. In *Skills, wages, and productivity in the service sector*, ed. T. Noyelle. Boulder: Westview Press, 1990.

Noyelle, T. J. and T. M. Stanback, Jr. *The Economic Transformation of American Cities*. Totowa, NJ: Rowman and Allanheld Publishers, 1983.

Office of Technology Assessment (OTA). *Trade in services: exports and foreign revenues—summary*. Washington, DC:U.S. Government Printing Office, 1986.

Oregon Joint Legislative Committee on Trade and Economic Development. Declining Numbers of "Family Wage" Jobs: A Threat to Oregon's Economic Health? Staff Report, exec. officer, J. Cortwright, 1984.

Peck, J. E., and B. R. Shappell. The income impact of the shift to service industry: a case study. *Economic Development Review* 4(2):11–15, 1986.

Perry, C. S. Industrialization, income, and inequality: further considerations. *Rural Sociology* 45(1):139–46, 1980.

Phillips, W., Jr. Perspective on rural development in the 1980s. In *New dimensions in rural policy: building upon our heritage*. Studies prepared for the Subcommittee on Agriculture and Transportation of the Joint Economic Committee, 99th Congress, 2nd Session, 1986.

Plunkert, L. M. The 1980s: a decade of job growth and industry shifts. *Monthly Labor Review* Sept.:3–16, 1990.

Population Today (A. H.). A species in danger of evolution? *Population Today* 16(4):3–4, 1988.

Porterfield, S. L. The export potential of selected services-producing and manufacturing industries. Paper presented at the annual meeting for the American Agricultural Economics Association, 1989.

Porterfield, S. Service sector offers more jobs, lower pay. *Rural Development Perspectives* June–Sept.:2–7, 1990.

Porterfield, S. L., and C. Kassab. The spatial allocation of labor in producer service industries. Paper presented at the North American meeting of the Regional Science Association International, 1991.

Pred, A. On the spatial structure of organizations and the complexity of metropolitan interdependence. *Papers of the Regional Science Association* 35:115–42, 1975.

Pulver, G. C. *Community economic development strategies*. University of Wisconsin-Extension, Cooperative Extension Service, G3366, 1986a.

Pulver, G. C. Economic growth in rural America. In *New dimensions in rural policy: building upon our heritage*. Studies Prepared for the Subcommittee on Agriculture and

Transportation of the Joint Economic Committee, 99th Congress, 2nd Session, 1986b.

Pulver, G. C. Service-producing industries in economic development. Paper presented at the Seventh Conference on the Small City and Regional Development at the University of Wisconsin–Stevens Point, 1986c.

Riddle, D. I. *Service-led growth*. New York: Praeger Publishers, 1986.

Riddle, D. I. The role of the service sector in economic development: similarities and differences by development category. *The emerging service economy*, ed. O. Giarini. Oxford: Pergamon Press, 1987.

Rogers, D. L., B. F. Pendleton, W. J. Goudy, and R. O. Richards. Industrialization, income benefits, and the rural community. *Rural Sociology* 43(2):250–64, 1978.

Rosenthal, N. H. The shrinking middle class: myth or reality? *Monthly Labor Review* 108(3):3–10, 1985.

Ross, C. O. Organizational dimensions of metropolitan dominance: prominence in the network of corporate control, 1955–1975. *American Sociological Review* 52(April):258–67, 1987.

SAS Institute, Inc. *SAS user's guide: statistics, version 5*. Cary, NC: SAS Institute, Inc, 1985.

Sheather, S. J., and T. P. Hettmansperger. Estimating the standard error of robust regression estimates. University Park, PA: The Pennsylvania State University, Department of Statistics, Technical Reports and Preprints, Number 70, 1987.

Shelp, R. K. A novel strategy for economic revitalization. *Economic Development Review* Winter:24–31, 1985.

Simmie, J. M. Beyond the industrial city? *Journal of the American Planning Association* Winter:59–76, 1983.

Smith, D. M. Who gets what where, and how: a welfare focus for human geography. *Geography* 59:289–297, 1974.

Smith, S. M. Export orientation of nonmanufacturing businesses in nonmetropolitan communities. *American Journal of Agricultural Economics* 66(May):145–55, 1984.

Smith, S. M. The role and potential contributions of services in the rural economy. Unpublished paper.

Smith, S. M., and G. C. Pulver. Nonmanufacturing industry: a shift in job creation strategy for rural America. *AIDC Journal* 13(April):7–22, 1978.

Smith, S. M., and G. C. Pulver. Nonmanufacturing business as a growth alternative in nonmetropolitan areas. *Journal of Community Development Society* 12(1):33–47, 1981.

Stacey, N., and D. To. Adult education and training markets. In *Skills, wages, and productivity in the service sector*, ed. T. Noyelle. Boulder: Westview, 1990.

Stanback, T. M., Jr. The changing face of retailing. In *Skills, wages, and productivity in the service sector*, ed. T. Noyelle. Boulder: Westview, 1990.

Stanback, T. M., Jr., and T. J. Noyelle. *Cities in Transition*. Totowa,NJ: Allanheld, Osmun and Co., Publishers, Inc., 1982.

Stanback, T. M., Jr., and T. Noyelle. Productivity in services: a valid measure of economic performance. In *Skills, wages, and productivity in the service sector*, ed. T. Noyelle. Boulder: Westview, 1990.

Sternlieb, G., and J. W. Hughes. Prologue: prelude to an agenda. In *Revitalizing the Northeast*, ed. G. Sternlieb and J. W. Hughes. New Brunswick, NJ: Center for Urban Policy Research, 1978.

Sternlieb, G., and J. W. Hughes. *Income and jobs: USA*. New Brunswick, NJ: Center for Urban Policy Research, 1984.

Stine, R. An introduction to bootstrap methods: examples and ideas. *Sociological Methods and Research* 18(2, 3):243–91, 1989.

Summers, G. F., S. D. Evans, F. Clemente, E. M. Beck, J. Minkoff. *Industrial invasion of nonmetropolitan America: a quarter century of experience*. New York: Praeger Publishers, 1976.

Tigges, L. M., and D. M. Tootle. Labor supply, labor demand, and men's underemployment in rural and urban labor markets. *Rural Sociology* 55(3):307–320, 1990.

Till, T. E. Industrialization and poverty in southern nonmetropolitan labor markets. *Growth and Change* 5(Jan.):18–24, 1974.

Till, T. E. Manufacturing industry: trends and impacts. In *Nonmetropolitan America in transition*, ed. A. H. Hawley and S. M. Mazie. Chapel Hill: The University of North Carolina Press, 1981.

Tolbert, C. M., II and M. S. Killian. *Labor market areas for the United States*. Washington, DC: U.S. Department of Agriculture, Economic Research Service, Staff Report No. AGES870721. 1987.

Tschetter, J. Producer services industries: why are they growing so rapidly? *Monthly Labor Review* 100(12): 31–40, 1987.

U.S. Bureau of the Census. *1970 Census user's guide*. U.S. Government Printing Office: Washington, DC, 1970.

U.S. Bureau of the Census. *Census of population: 1970 general social and economic characteristics*. Washington, D.C.: U.S. Government Printing Office, 1972.

U.S. Bureau of the Census. *Vol. 1, Characteristics of the population United States summary—section 1*. Washington, DC: U.S. Government Printing Office, 1973.

U.S. Bureau of the Census. *Statistical abstract of the United States: 1963*. 84th ed. Washington, DC: U.S. Government Printing Office, 1963.

U.S. Bureau of the Census. *Statistical abstract of the United States: 1980*. 100th ed. Washington, DC: U.S. Government Printing Office, 1980.

U.S. Bureau of the Census. *Statistical abstract of the United States: 1981*. 101th ed. Washington, DC: U.S. Government Printing Office, 1981.

U.S. Bureau of the Census. *1980 Census of population and housing. User's guide, part b—glossary*. Washington, DC: U.S. Government Printing Office, 1982a.

U.S. Bureau of the Census. *County Business Patterns, 1974–1980: technical documentation*. Washington, DC: U.S. Government Printing Office, 1982b.

U.S. Bureau of the Census. *Vol. 1, characteristics of the population part 1, United States summary*. Washington, DC: U.S. Government Printing Office, 1983.

U.S. Bureau of the Census. *Statistical abstract of the United States: 1985*. 105th ed. Washington, DC: U.S. Government Printing Office, 1985.

U.S. Bureau of the Census. *Statistical abstract of the United States: 1986*. 106th ed. Washington, DC: U.S. Government Printing Office, 1985.

U.S. Bureau of the Census. *Statistical abstract of the United States: 1987*. 107th ed. Washington, DC: U.S. Government Printing Office, 1987.

U.S. Bureau of the Census. *Statistical abstract of the United States: 1990*. 110th ed. Washington, DC: U.S. Government Printing Office, 1990.

U.S. Department of Labor. *Employment and earnings, states and areas, 1939–1978*. 1370–13, November Bulletin, 1979.

U.S. Department of Labor. *News: multiple jobholding reached record high in May 1989.*
    USDL 89–529, November 6, 1989.

U.S. General Accounting Office (GAO). *Workers at risk: increased numbers in contingent
    employment lack insurance, other benefits.* GAO/HRD-91–56, 1991.

Urquhart, M. The employment shift to services: where did it come from? *Monthly Labor
    Review* 107(4):15–22, 1984.

Warner, W. K. Rural society in a post-industrial age. *Rural Sociology* 39(Fall):307–18,
    1974.

Watkins, A. J., and D. C. Perry. Regional change and the impact of uneven urban devel-
    opment. In *The Rise of the Sunbelt Cities*, ed. D.C. Perry and A. J. Watkins. Bev-
    erly Hills: Sage Publications, 1977.

Wilkinson, K. P. Social well-being and community. *Journal of the Community Develop-
    ment Society* 10(1):5–16, 1979.

Young, F. W. *Interdisciplinary Theories of Rural Development.* Greenwich, CT: JAI
    Press, Inc, 1983.

Index

About the Author

CATHY KASSAB is a research associate with the Center for Health Policy Research at The Pennsylvania State University.